ROUSSEAU RECONSTRUCTED  PAUL

"One who knows how to appreciate color relationships, the influence of one color with another, their contrasts and dissonances, is promised an infinite variety of images."
Sonia Delaunay

"The actual basis of colour is instability. Once you accept that in lieu of something which is stable, which is form, you are dealing with something which is unstable in its basic character, you begin to get a way of dealing with it."
Bridget Riley

"The sensations of colors on the palette can be spiritual experiences."
Wassily Kandinsky

"The more basic the color, the more inward, the more pure."
Piet Mondrian

"Color is the place where our brain and the universe meet."
Paul Klee

Author's Note

Each sequence in this book begins with a 1x1 pixel resolution (approximately 0.15 ppi [pixels per inch]) image created by reducing a digital file of the original painting. The image sequence continues with pixel resolutions of 3x3 (0.4 ppi), 7x7 (1 ppi), 15x15 (2.2 ppi), 31x31 (4.5 ppi), 63x63 (9.2 ppi), 127x127 (18.6 ppi), 255x255 (37.4 ppi), 511x511 (74.9 ppi), 1023x1023 (150 ppi), and 2047x2047 (300 ppi, the typically accepted "full resolution" printing standard).

The sequences are repeated at the end of the book in smaller one page, nine-image sequences with pixel resolutions of 1x1 (0.6 x ppi), 3x3 (1.7 x ppi), 7x7 (4.1 x ppi), 15x15 (8.8 x ppi), 31x31 (18.2 ppi), 63x63 (37 ppi), 127x127 (74.7 ppi), 255x255 (150 ppi), and 511x511 (300 ppi).

Each pixel represents an average color distribution over the corresponding area in the original painting, that is the 1x1 pixel images represent the average color distribution over the entire painting, the 3x3 pixels each represent 1/9th of the painting, the 7x7 pixels each represent 1/49th of the painting, and so on.

The featured paintings are cropped to fit the format of this book.

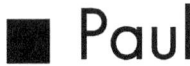 Paul

Boy on the Rocks

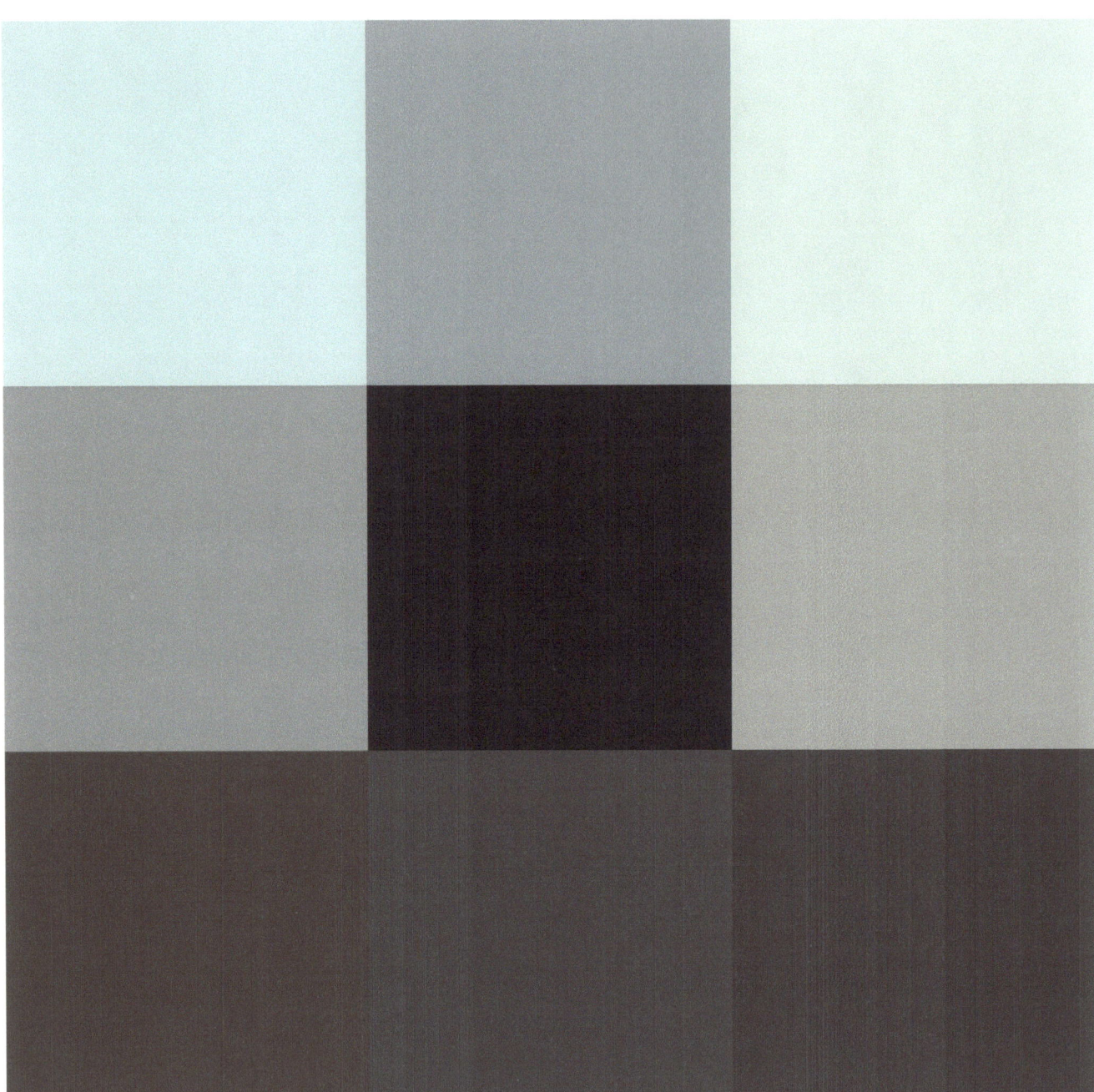

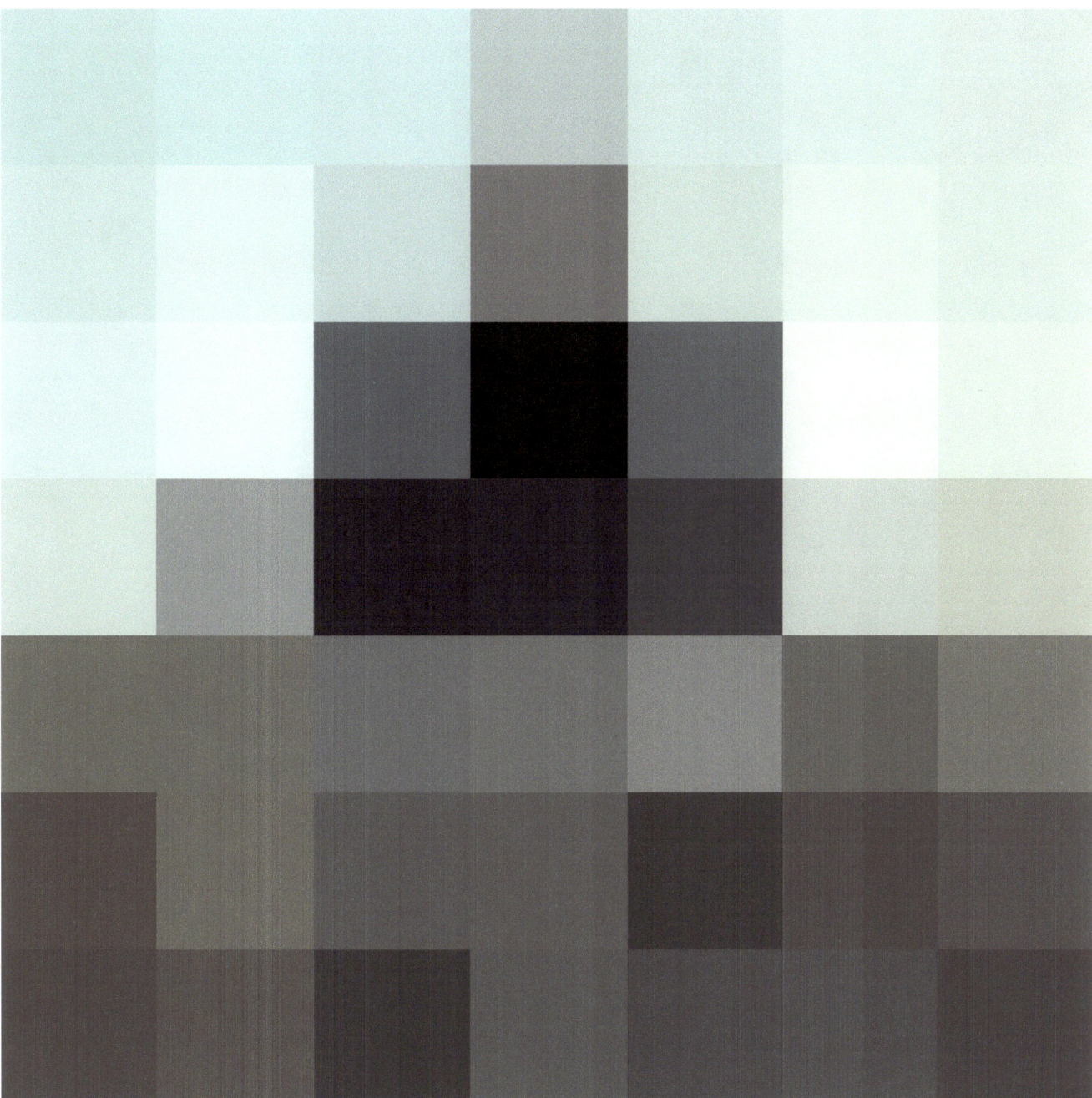

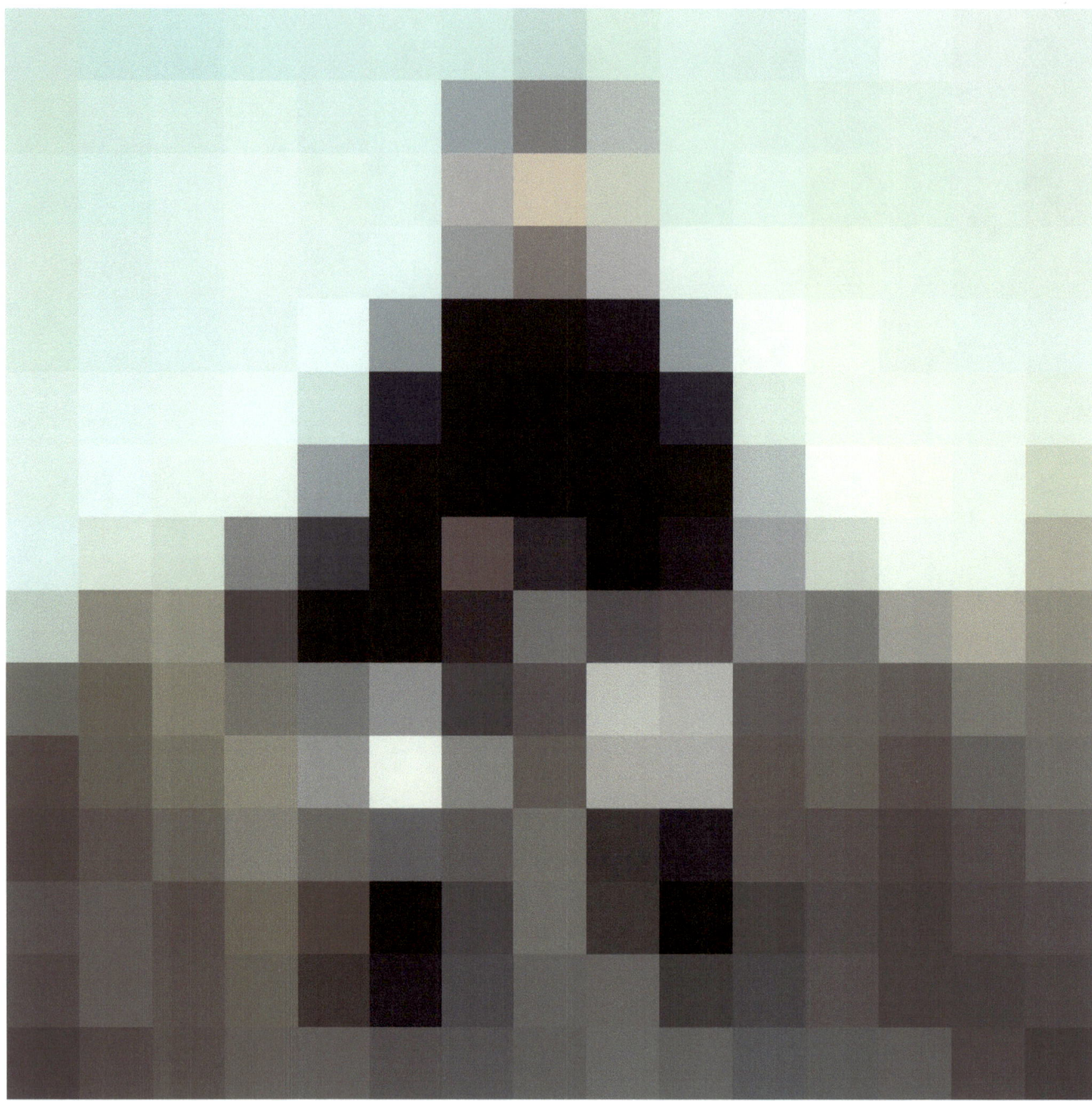

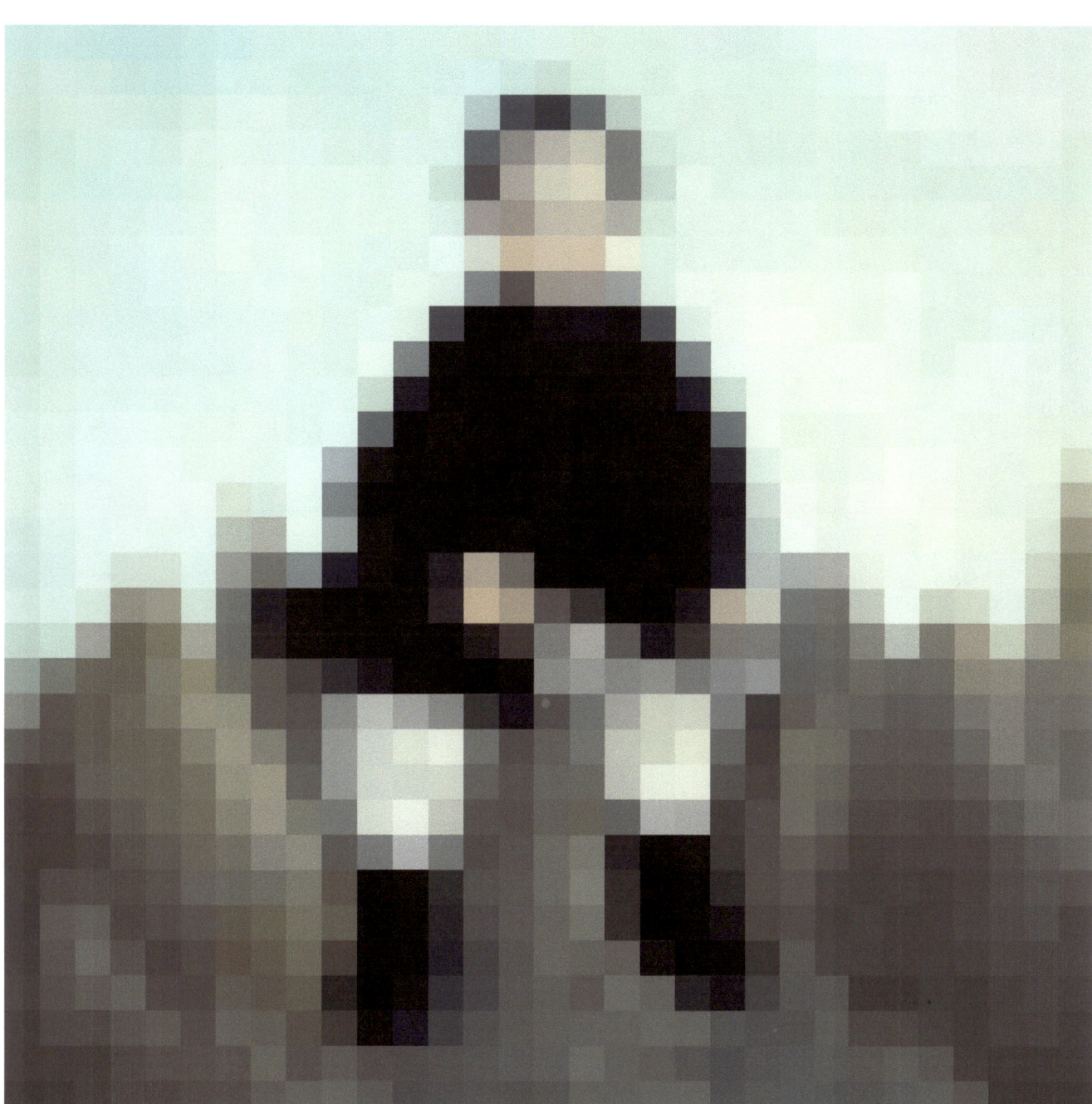

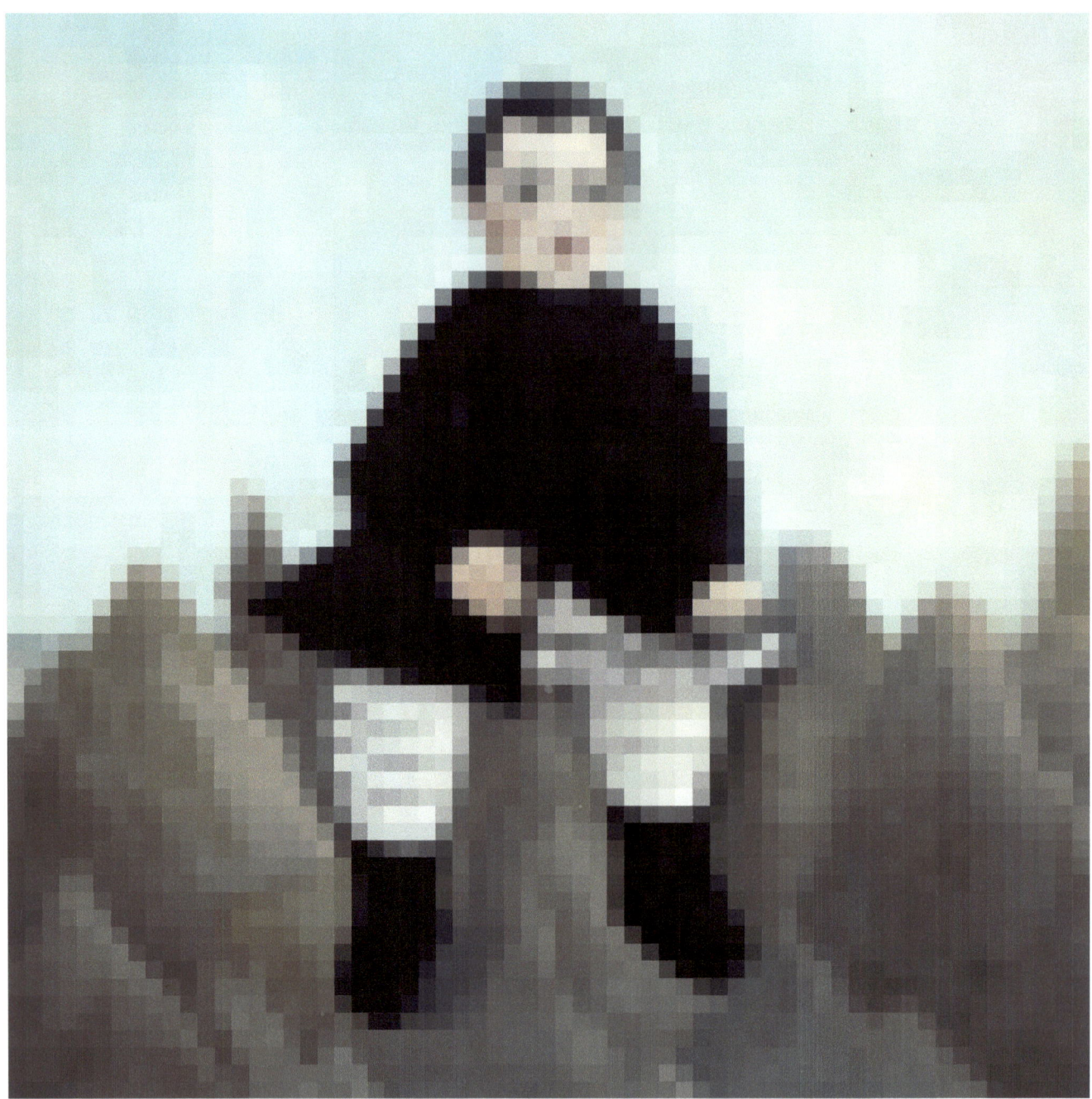

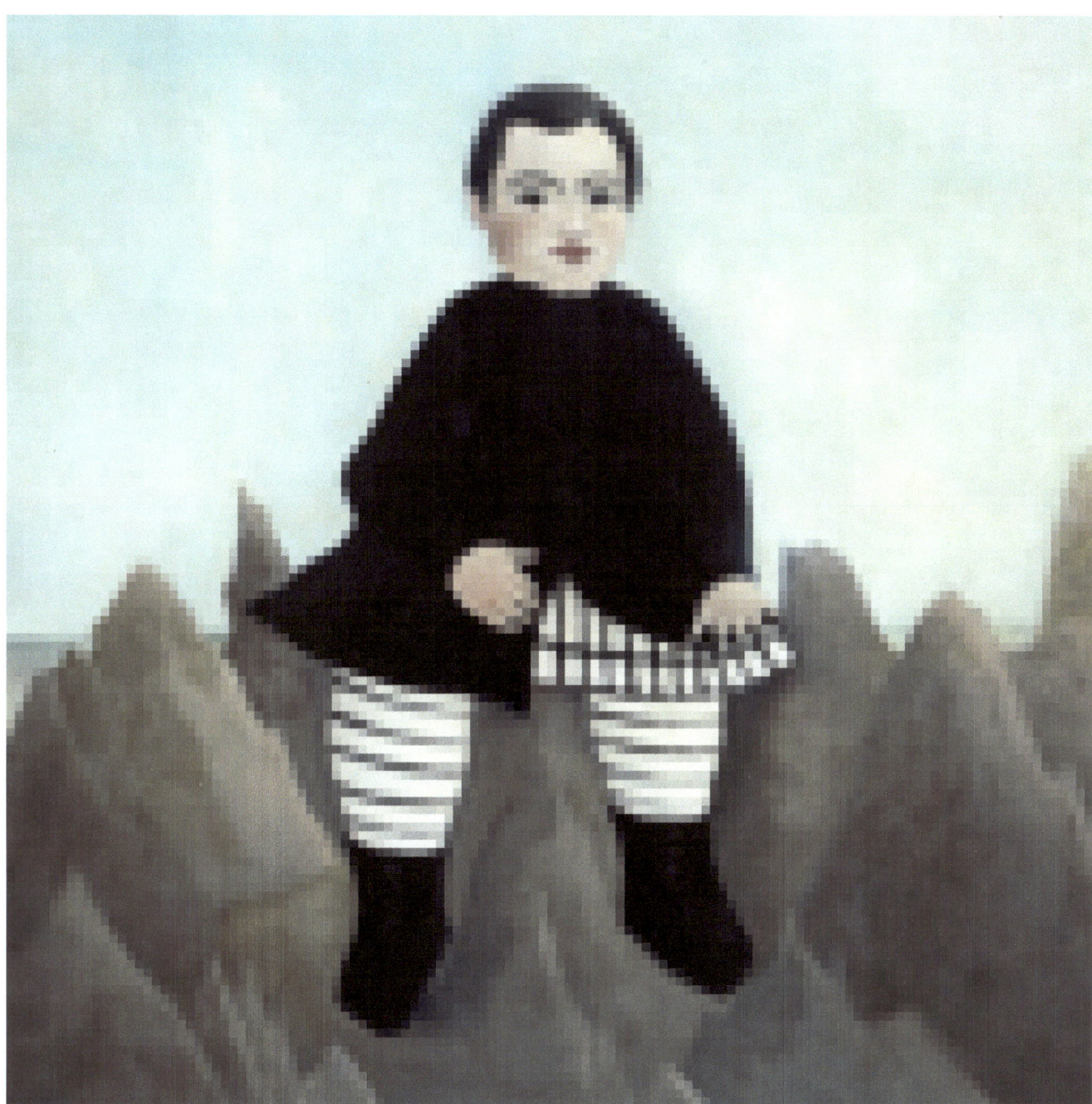

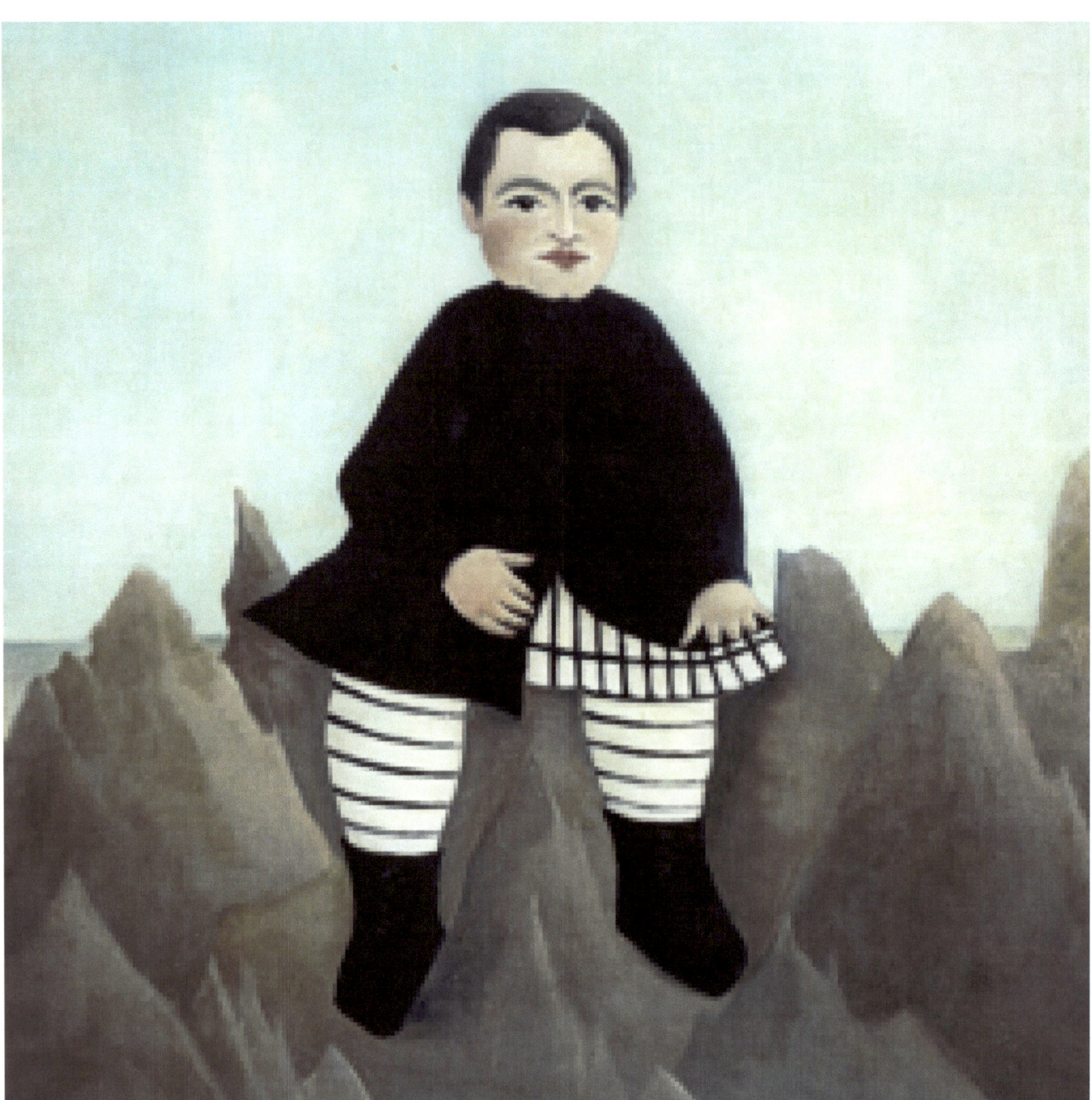

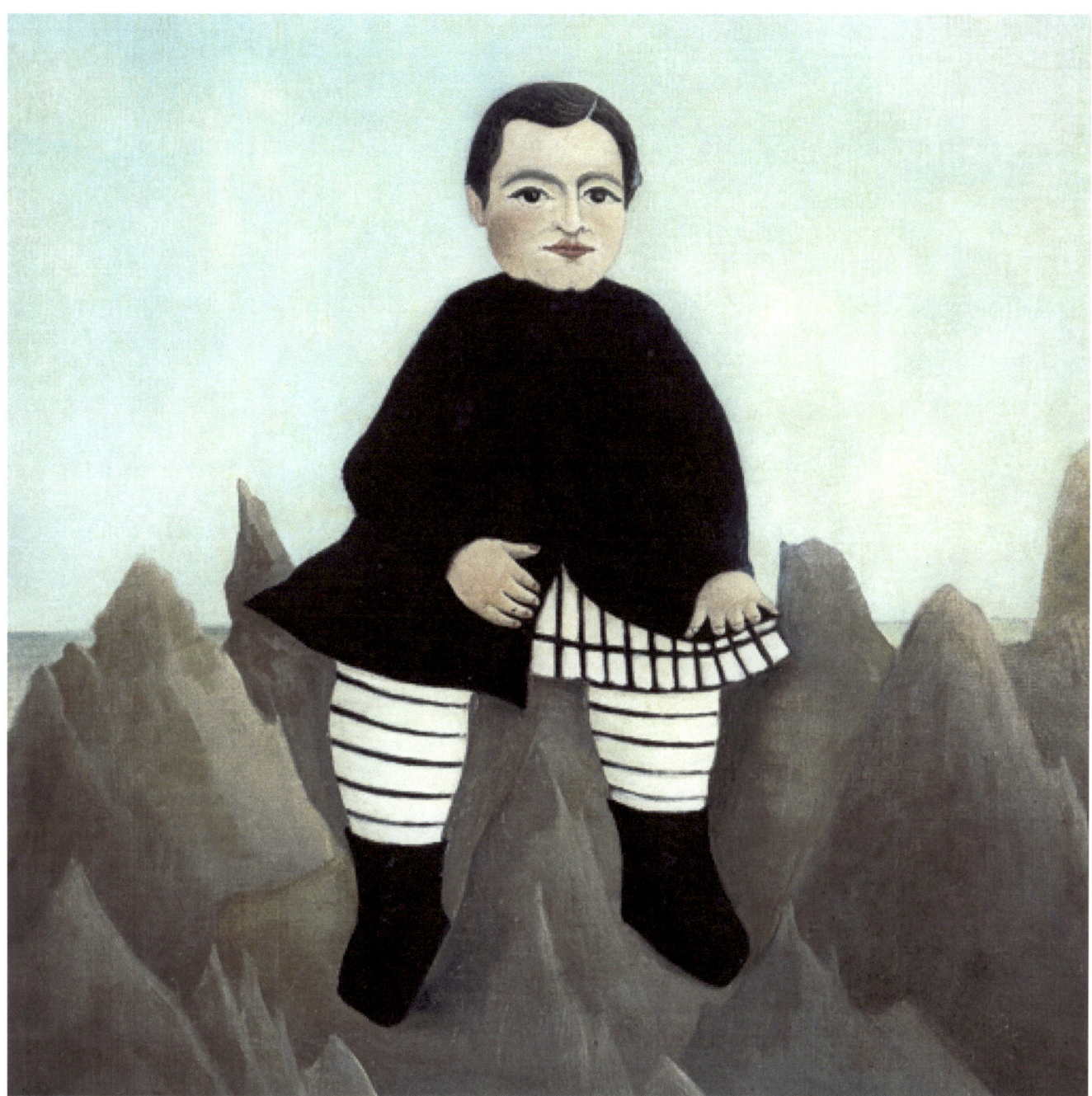

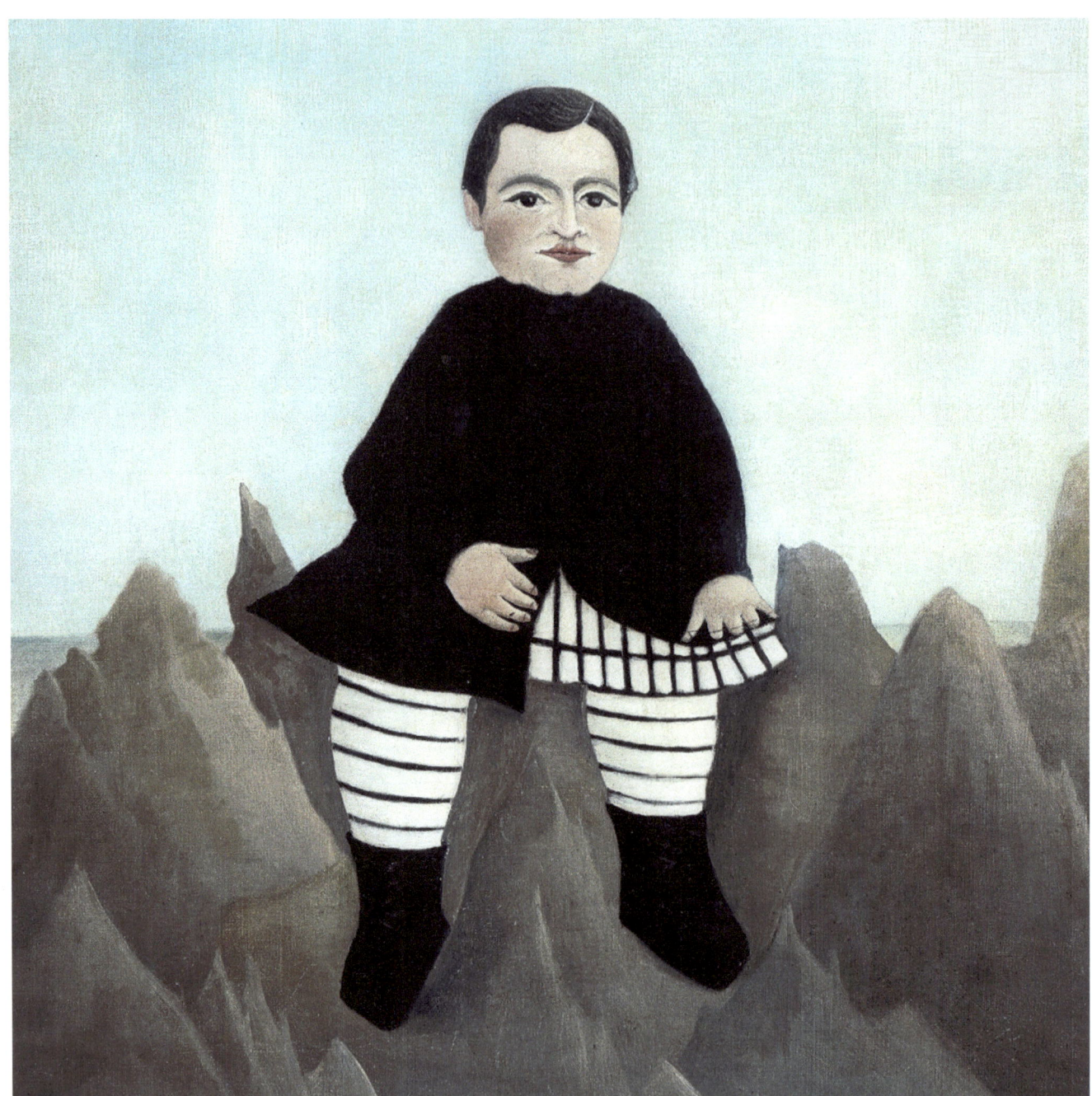

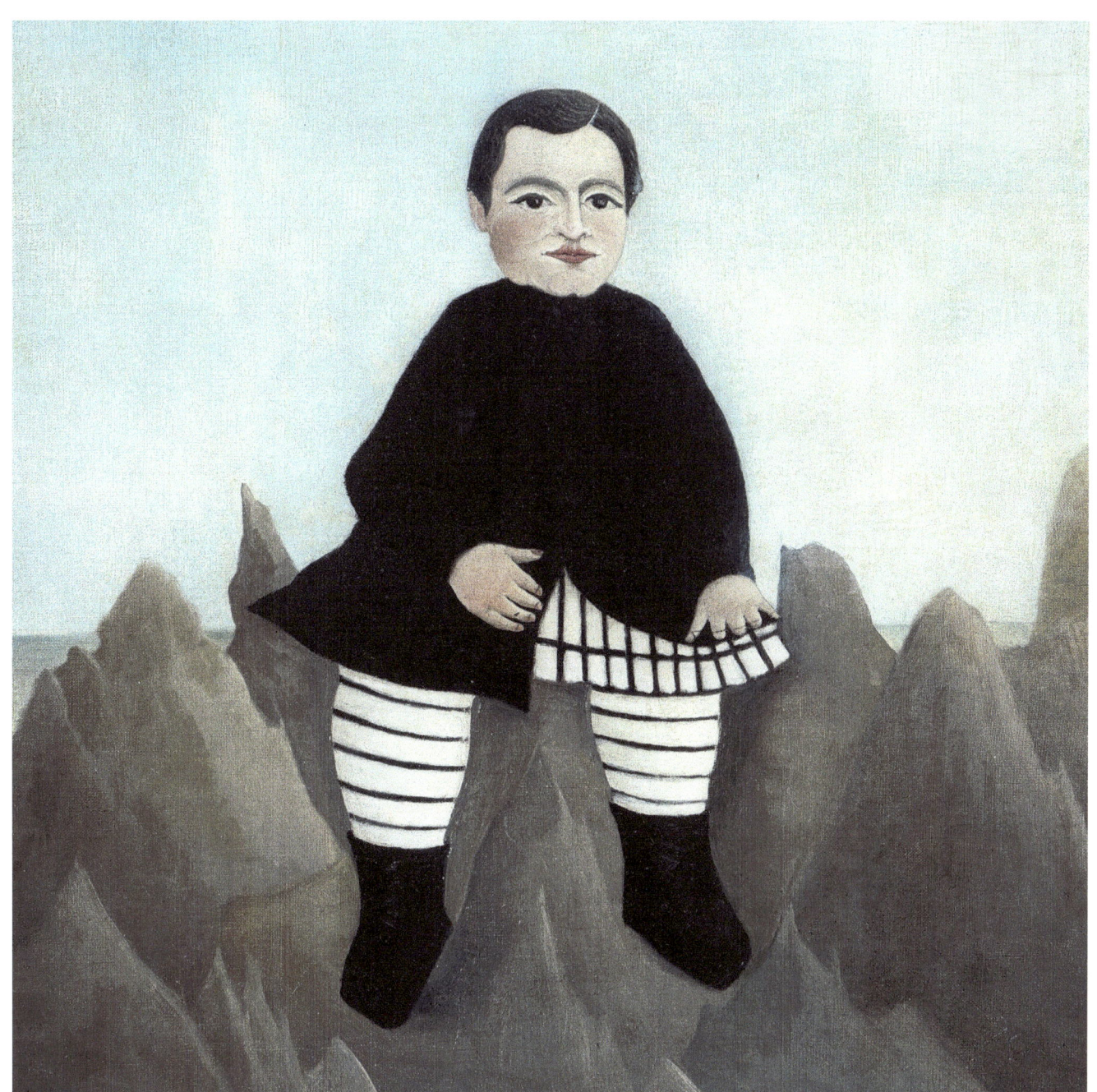

Self-Portrait

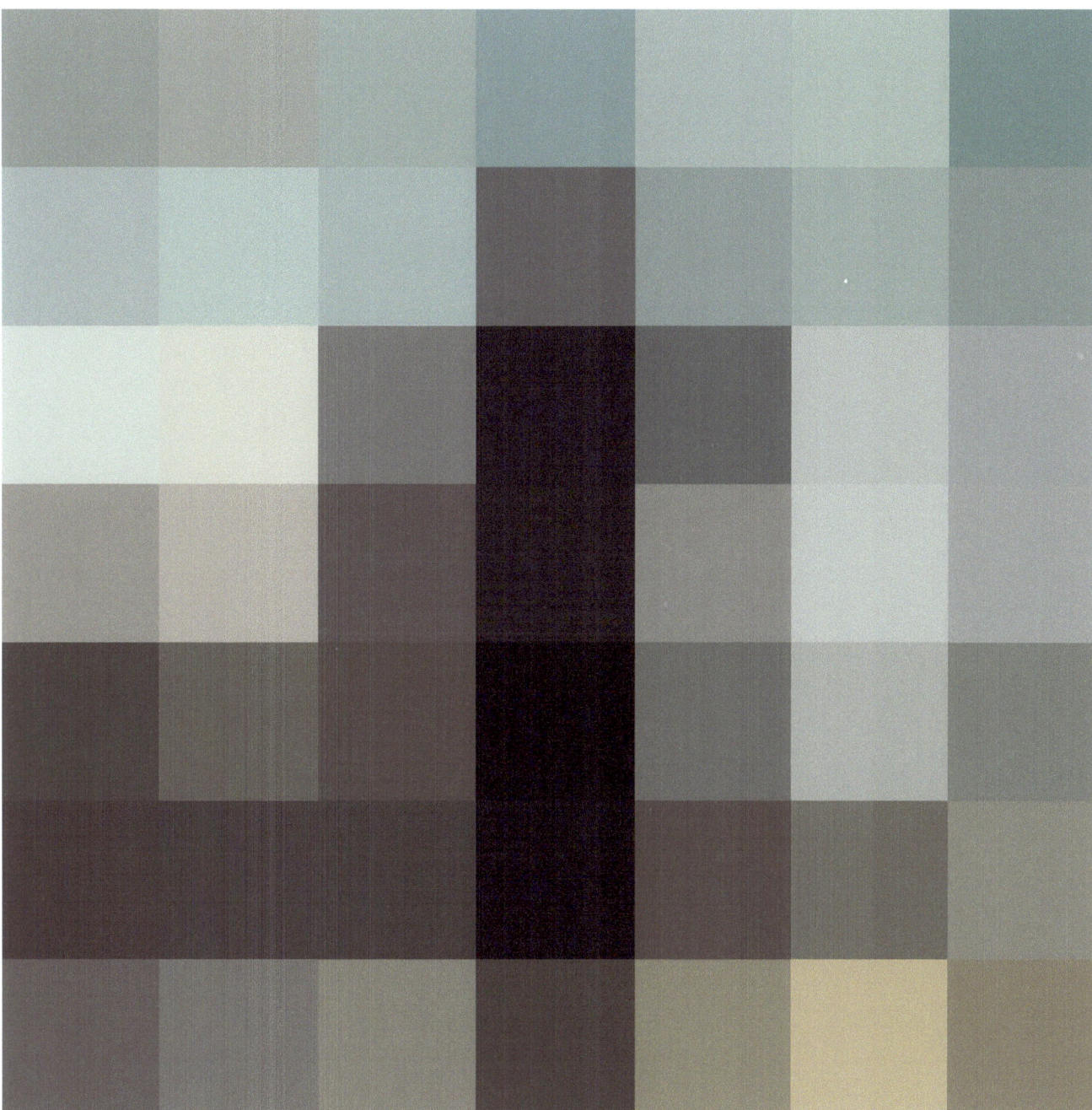

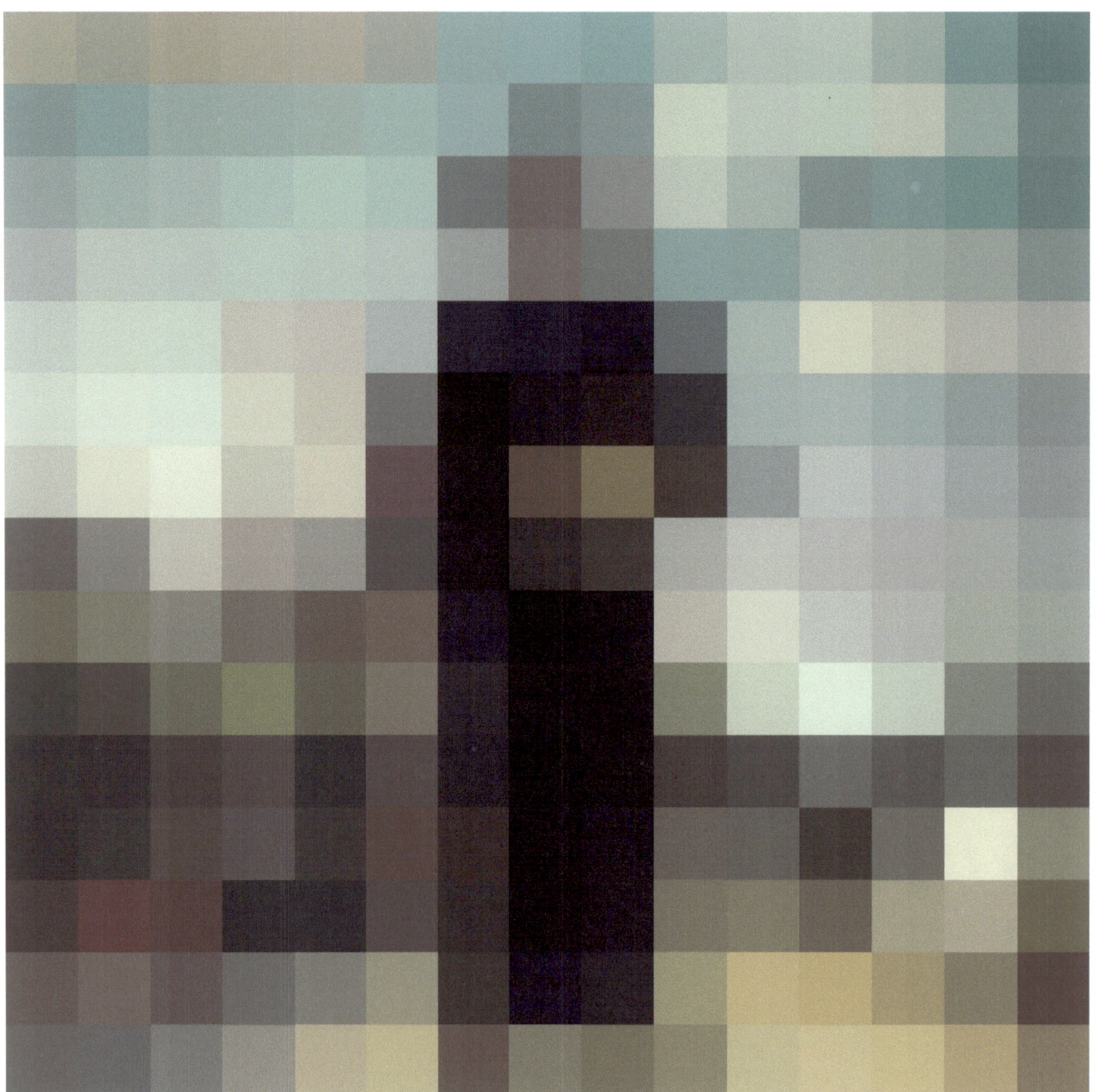

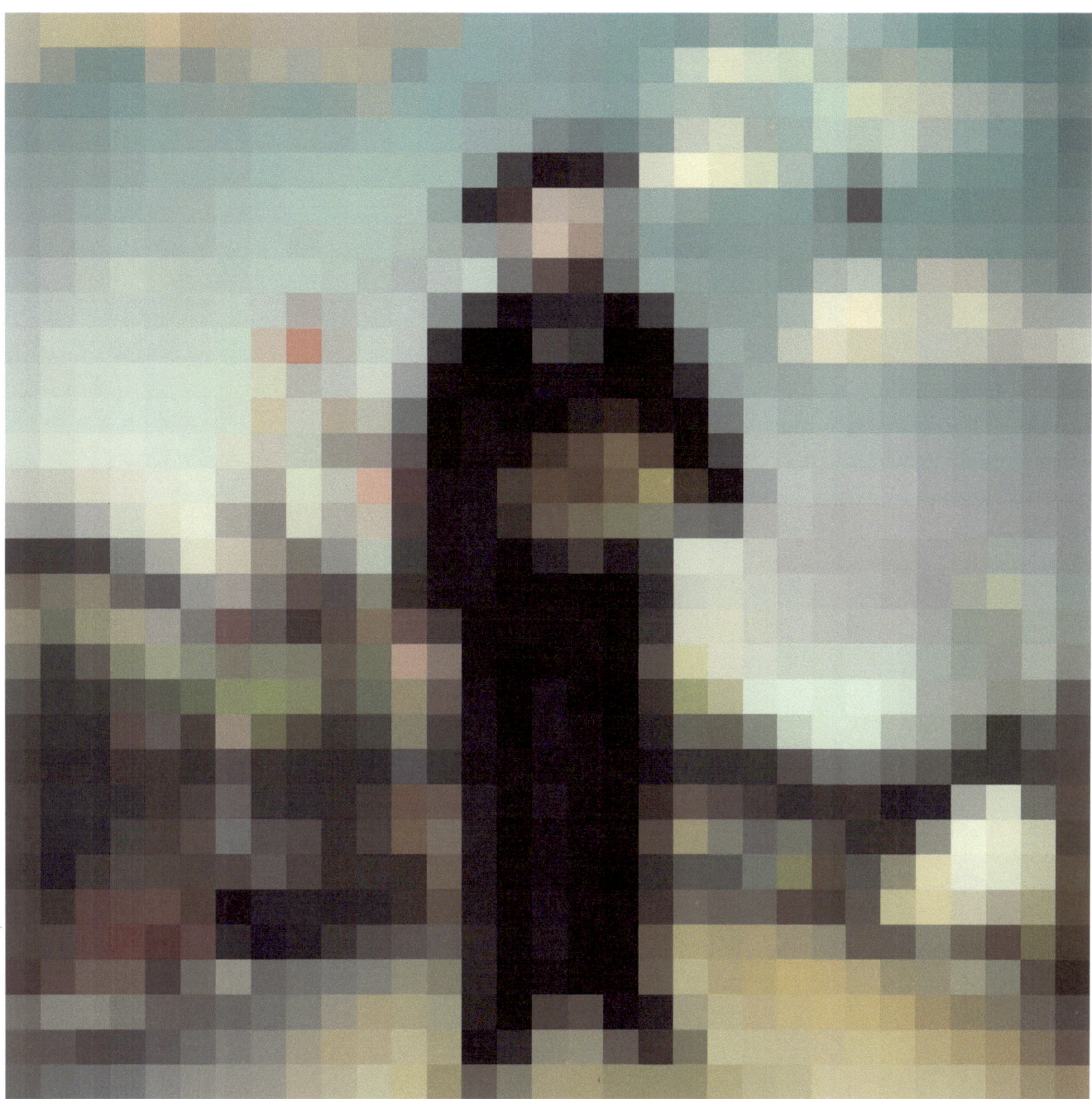

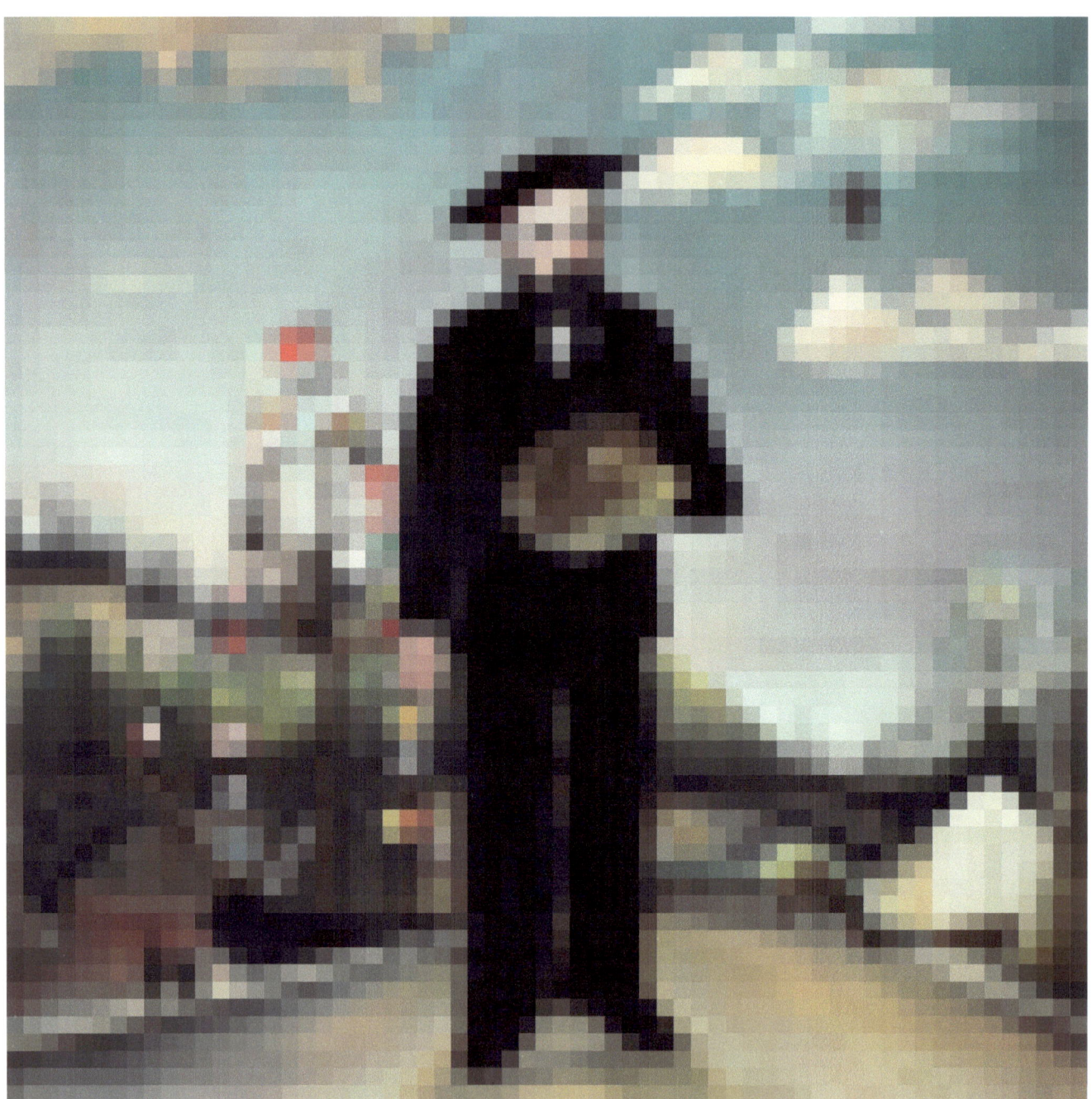

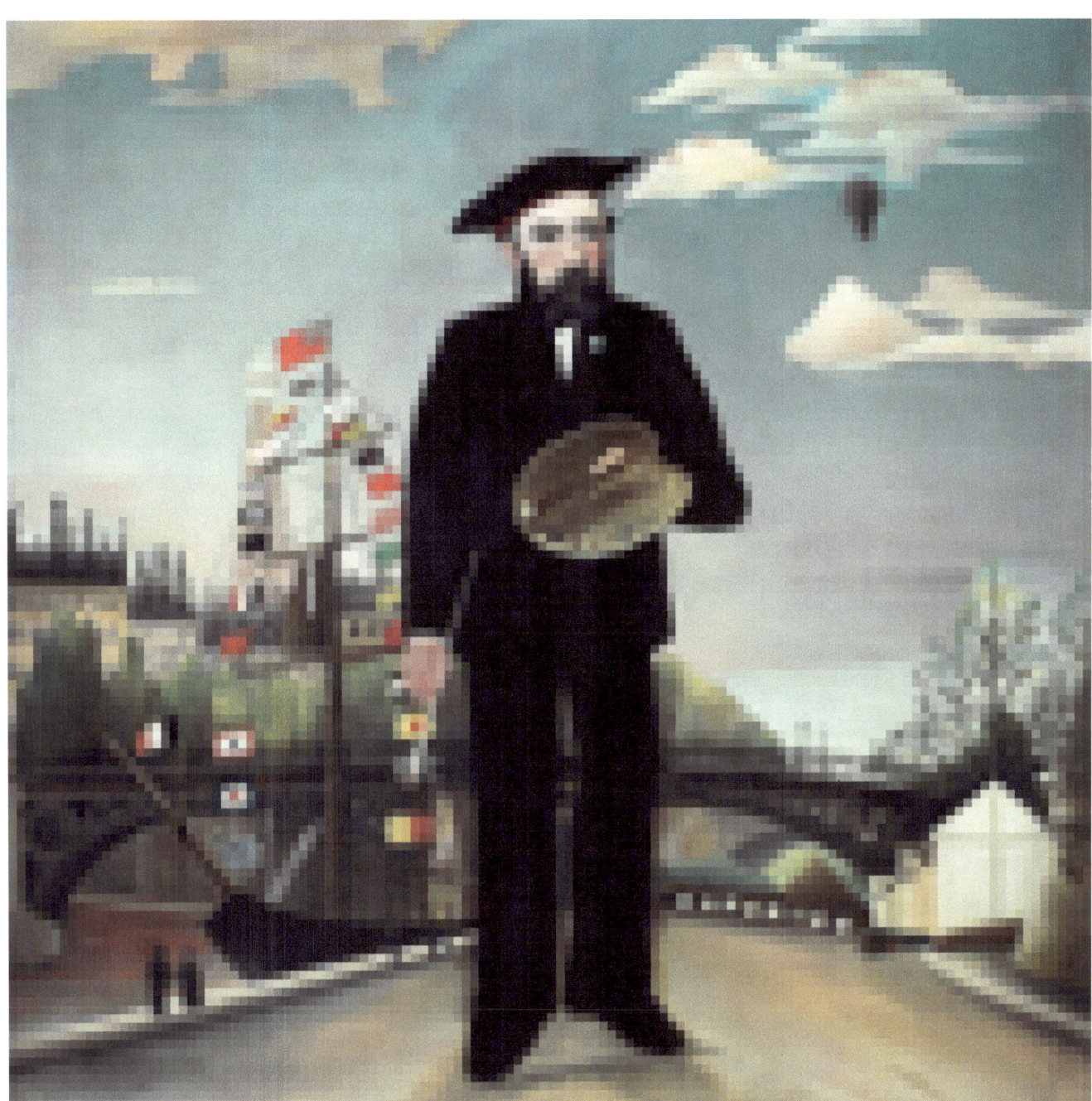

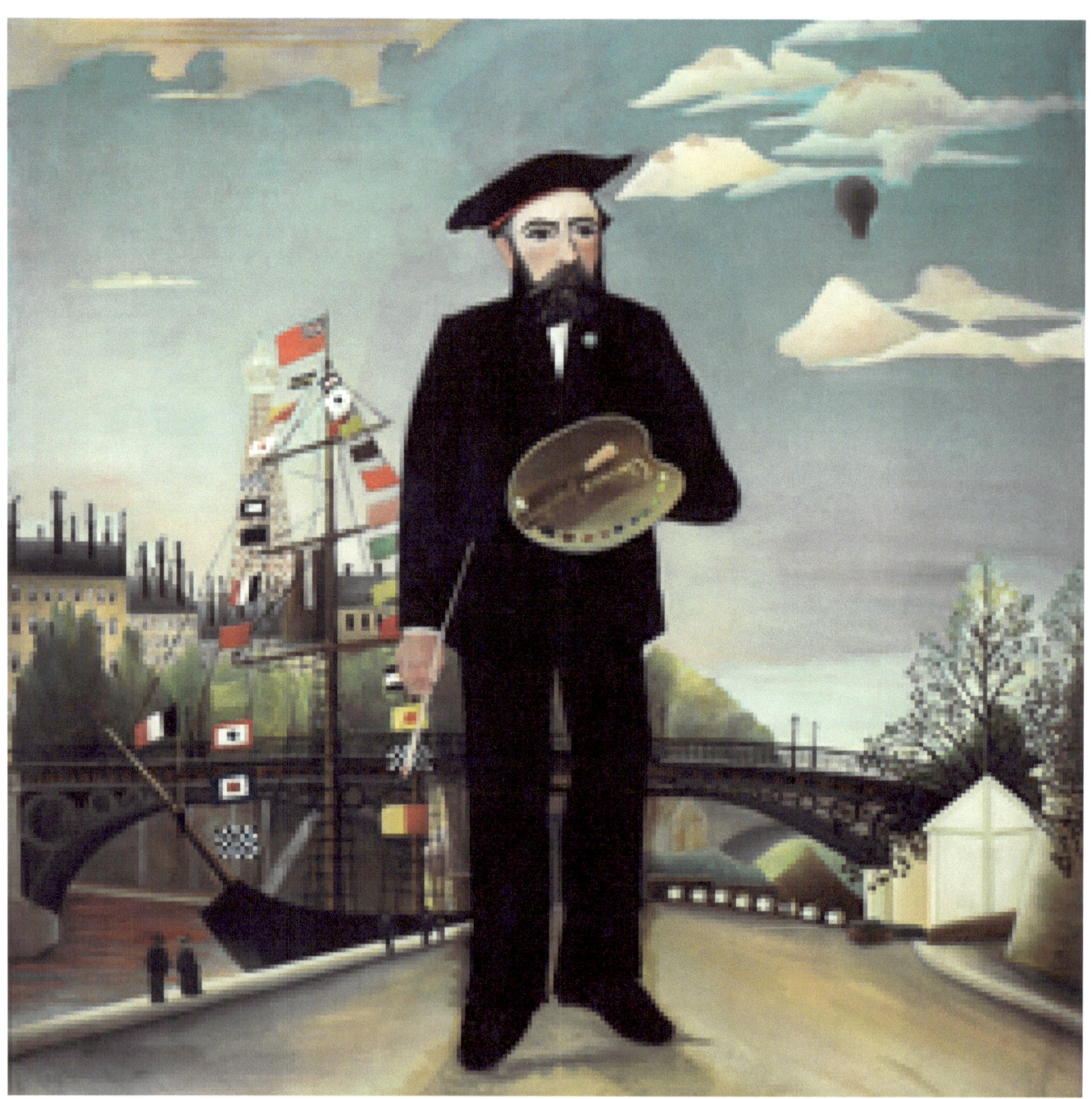

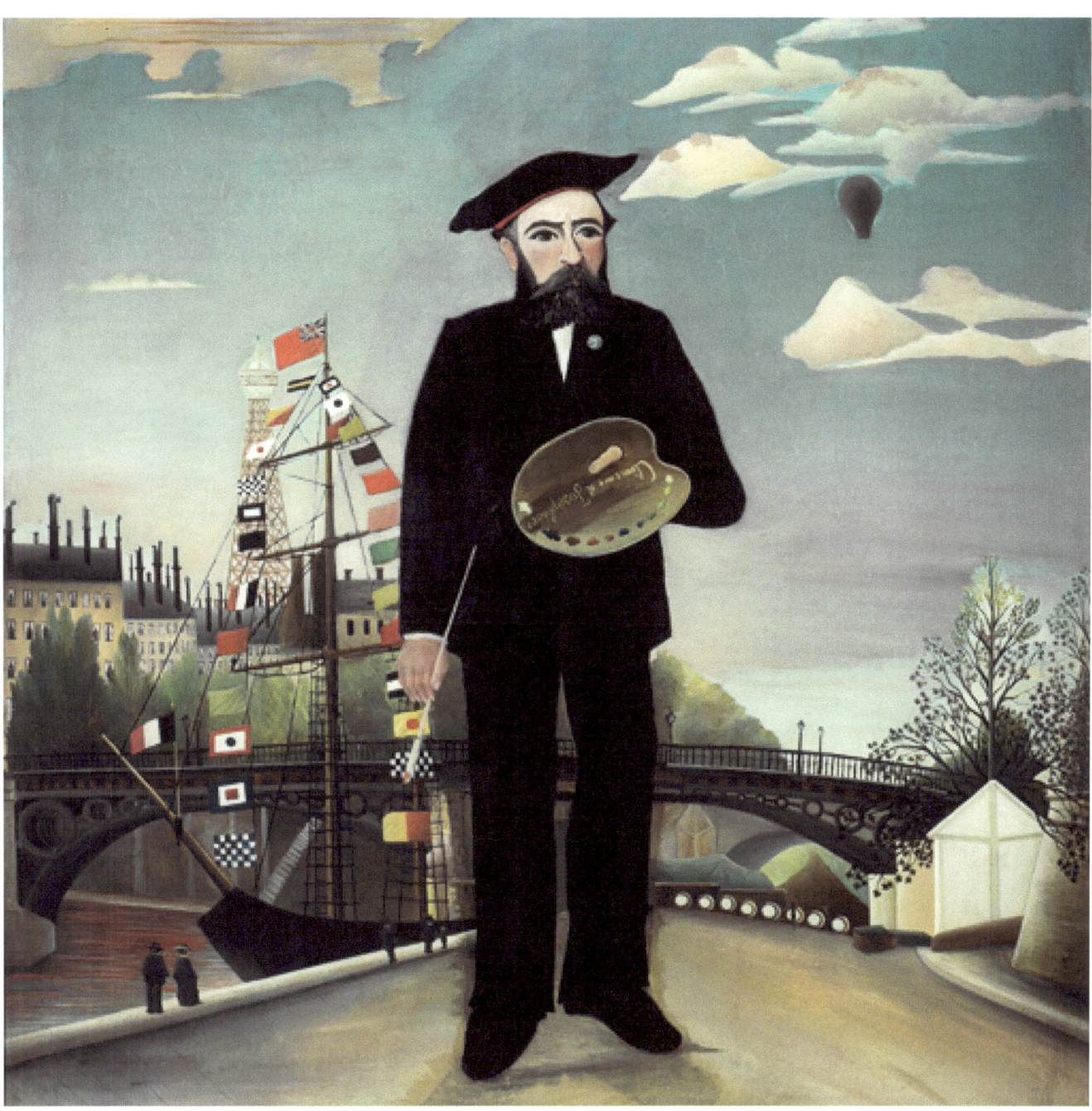

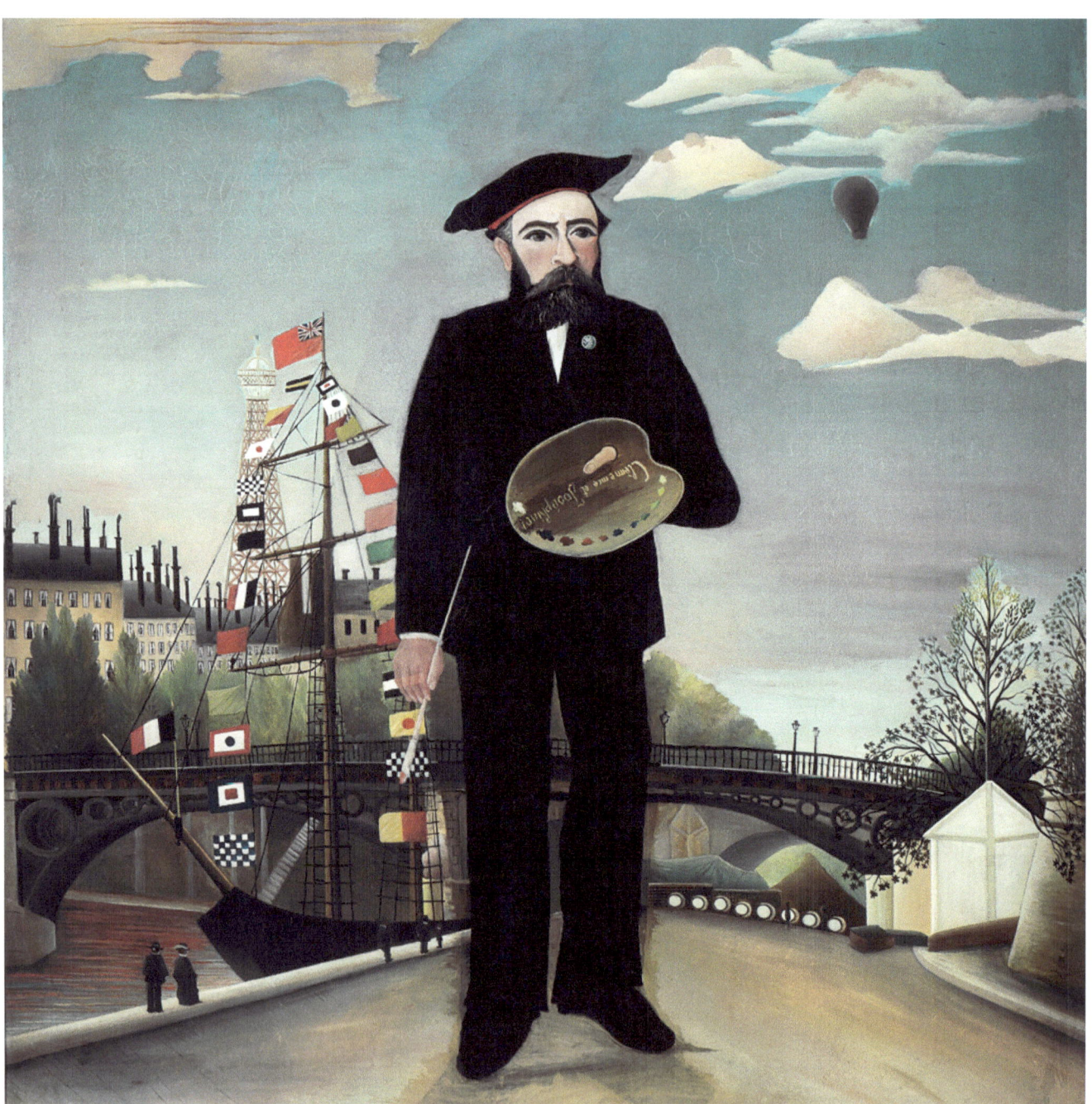

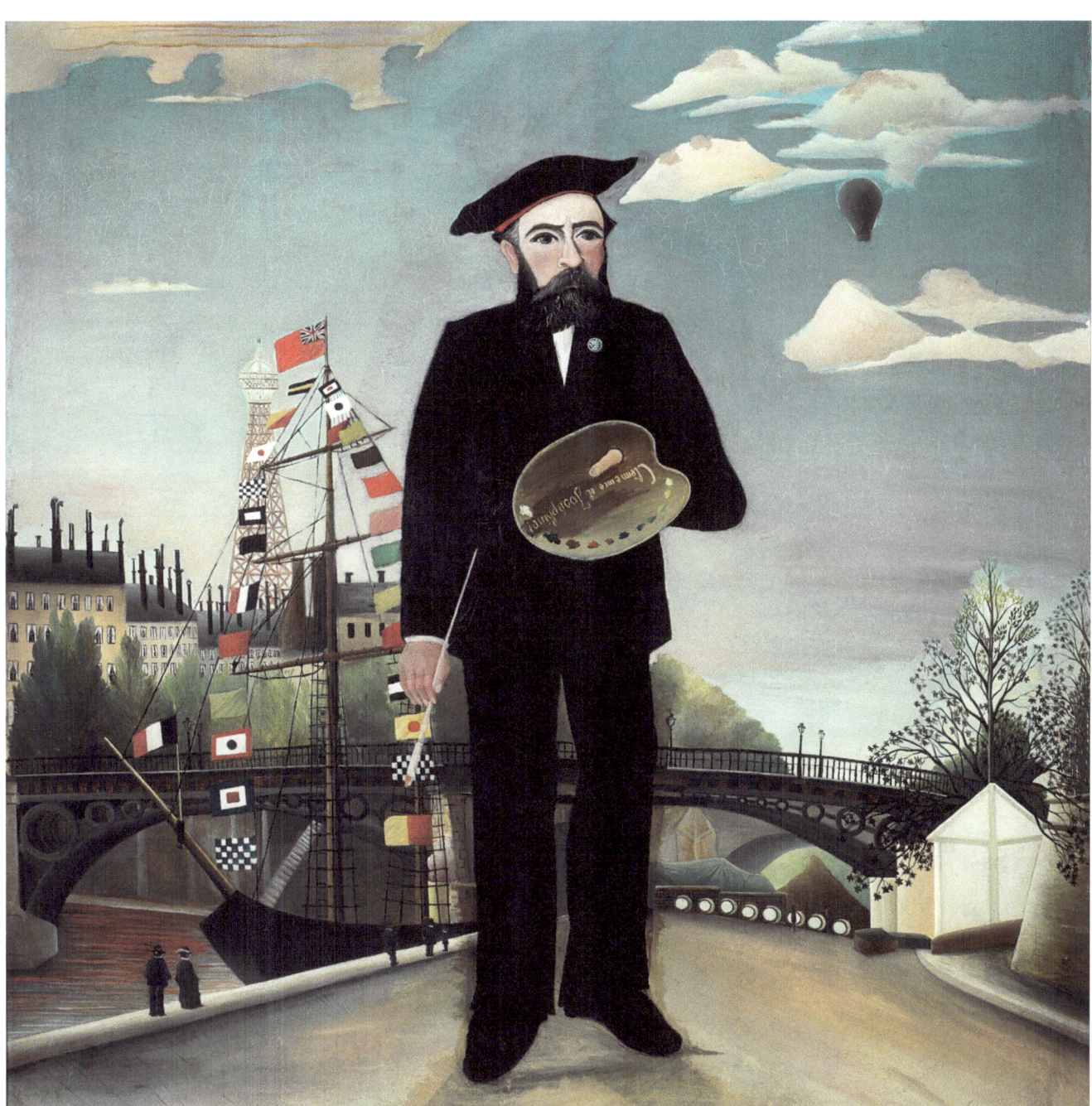

Fight between A Tiger
and A Bull

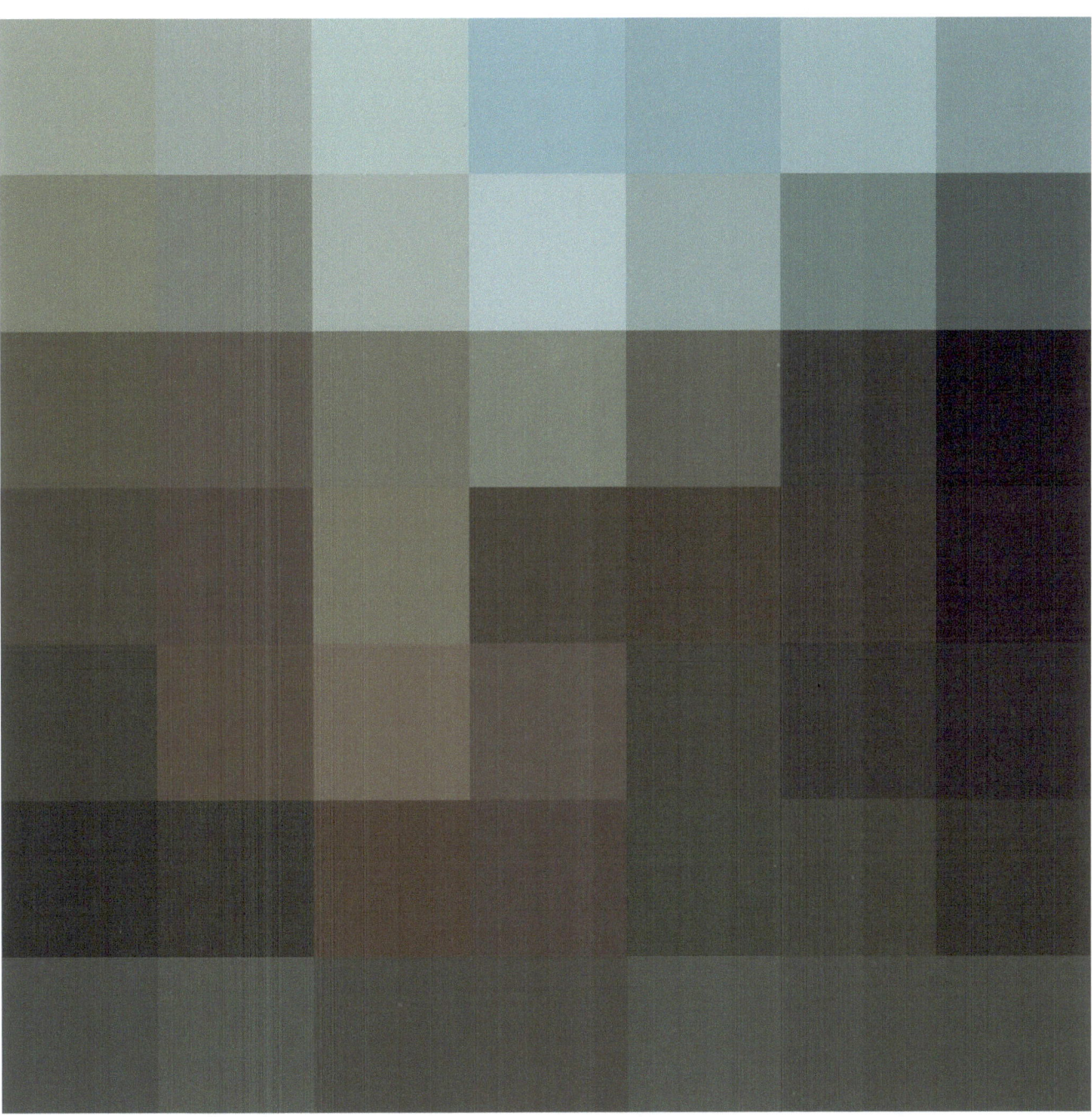

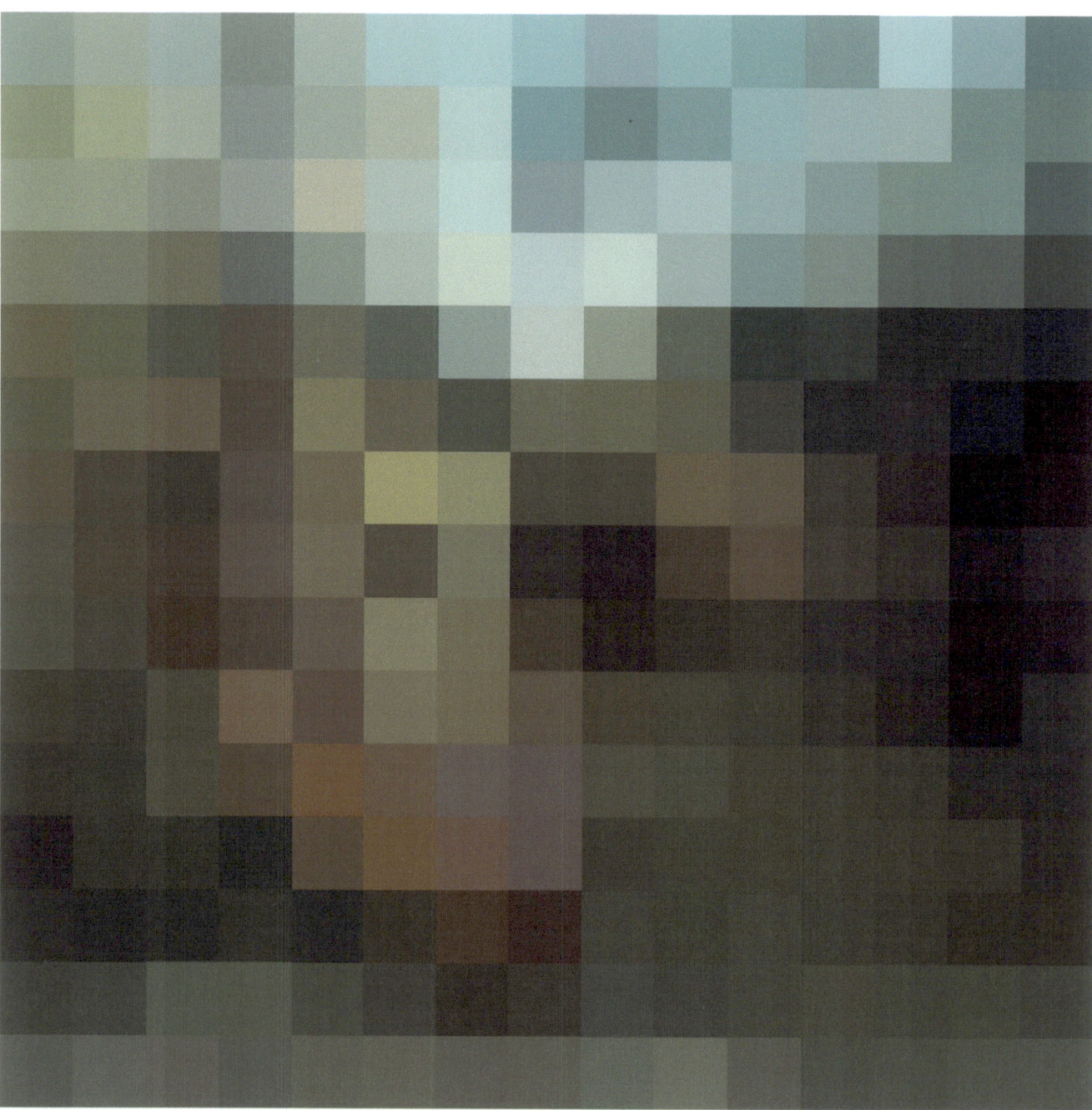

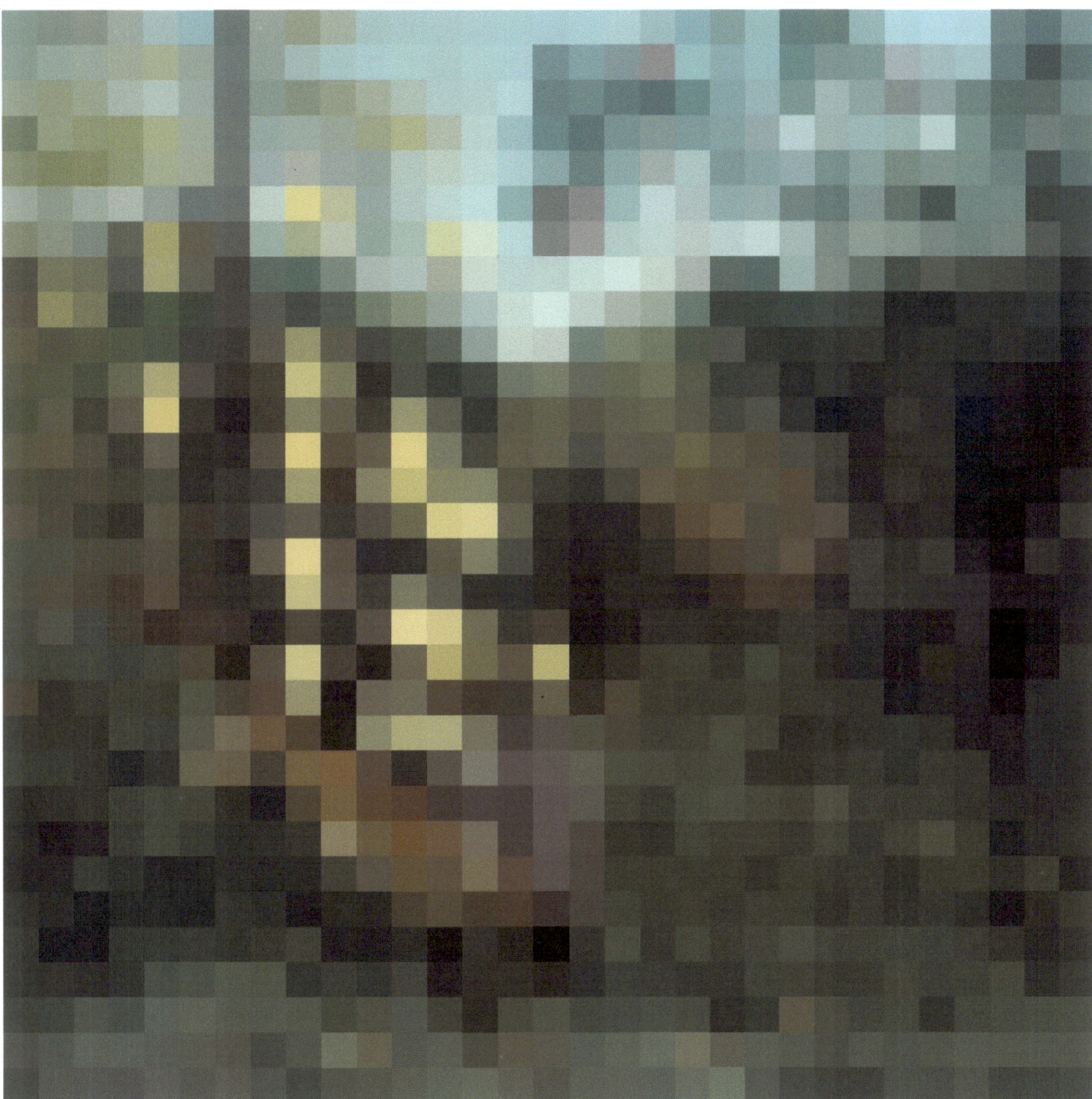

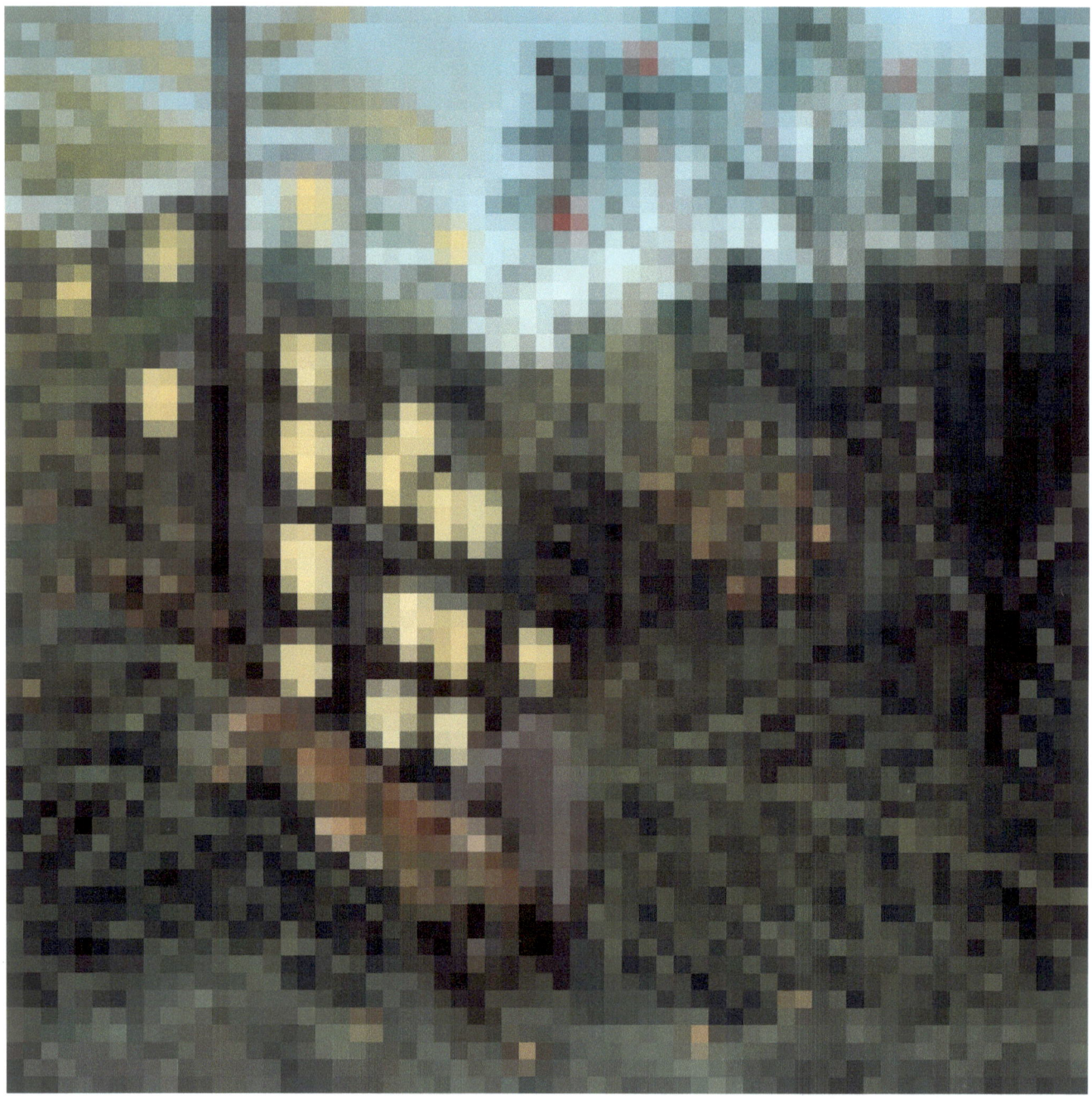

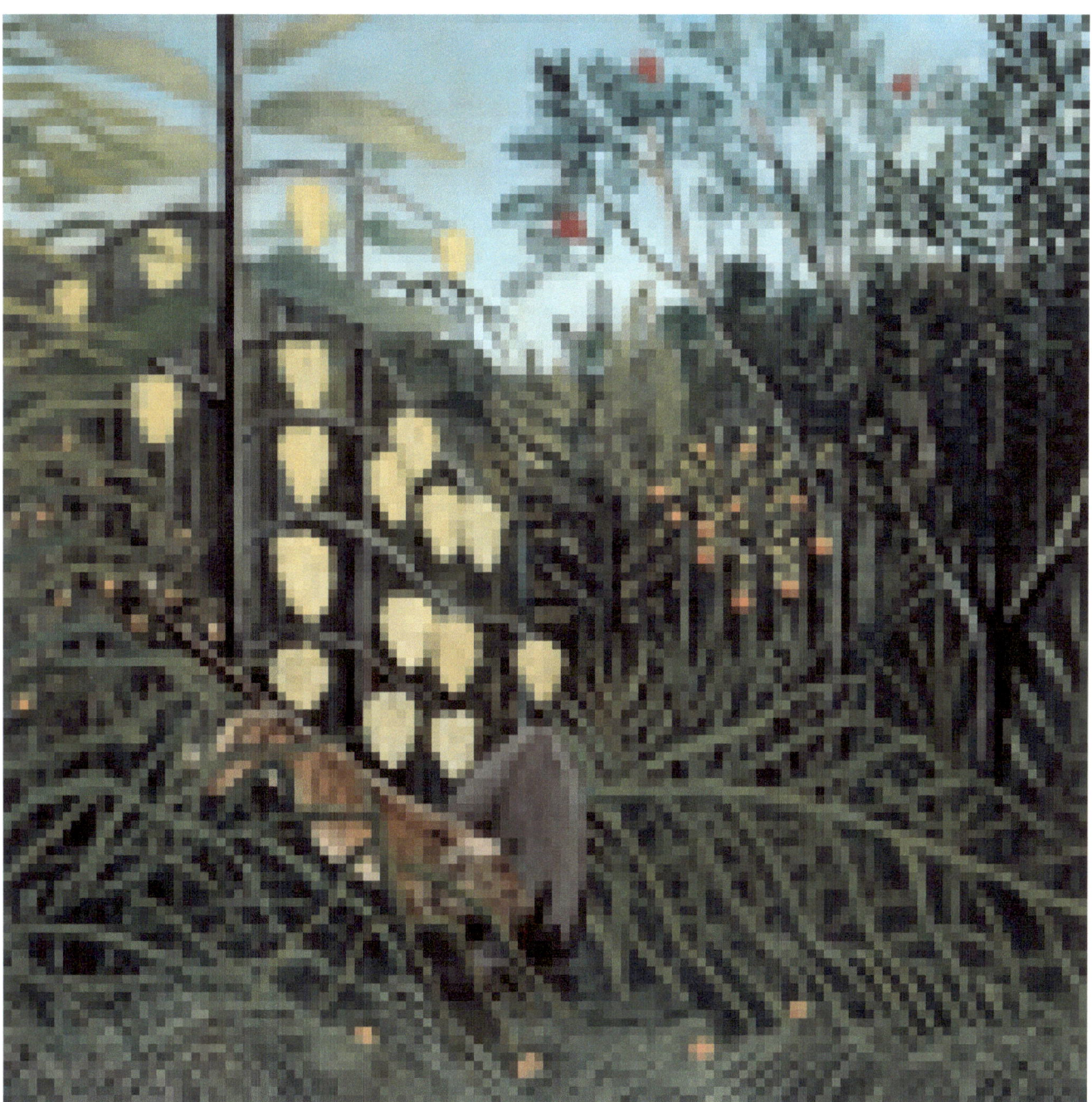

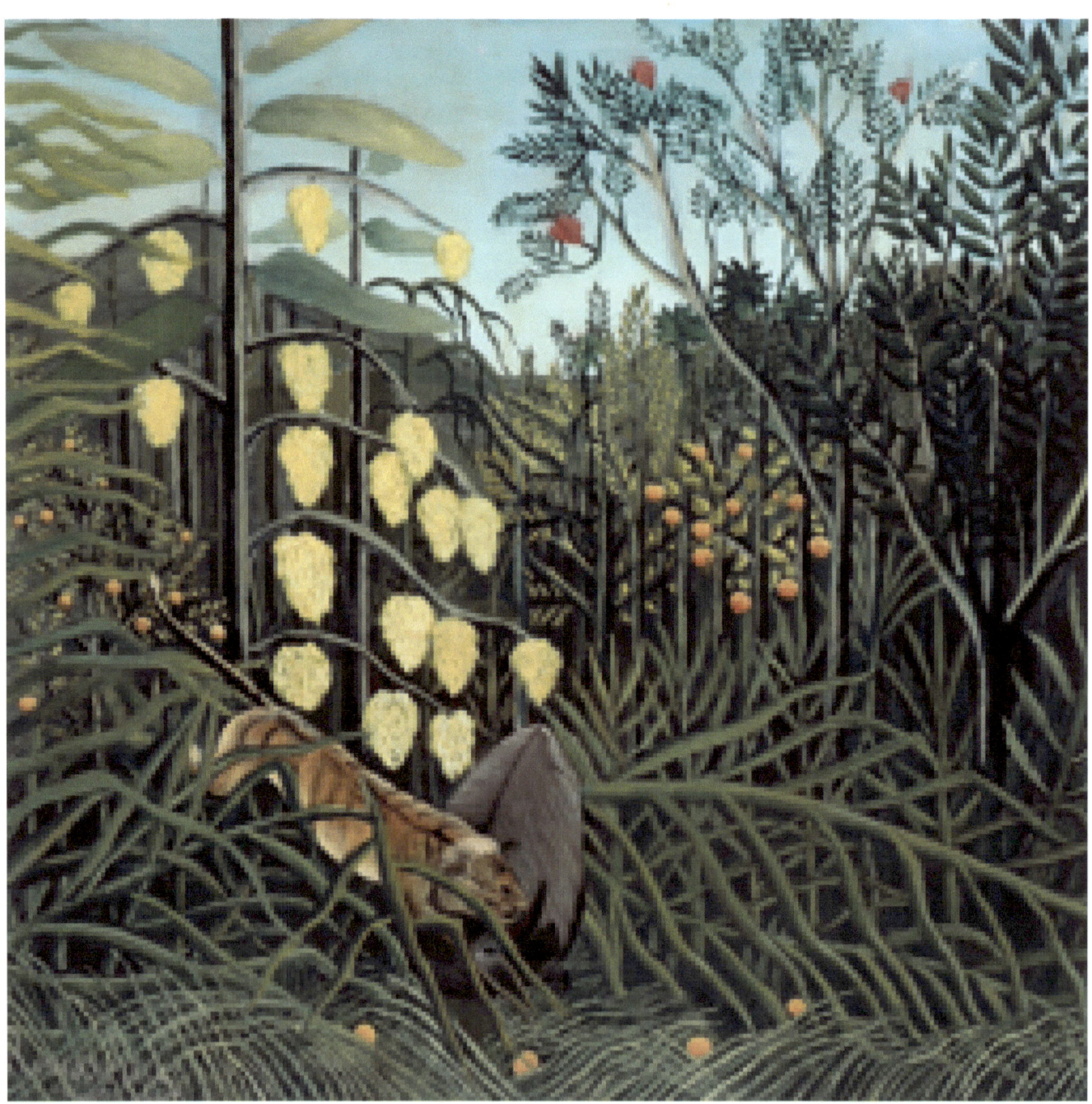

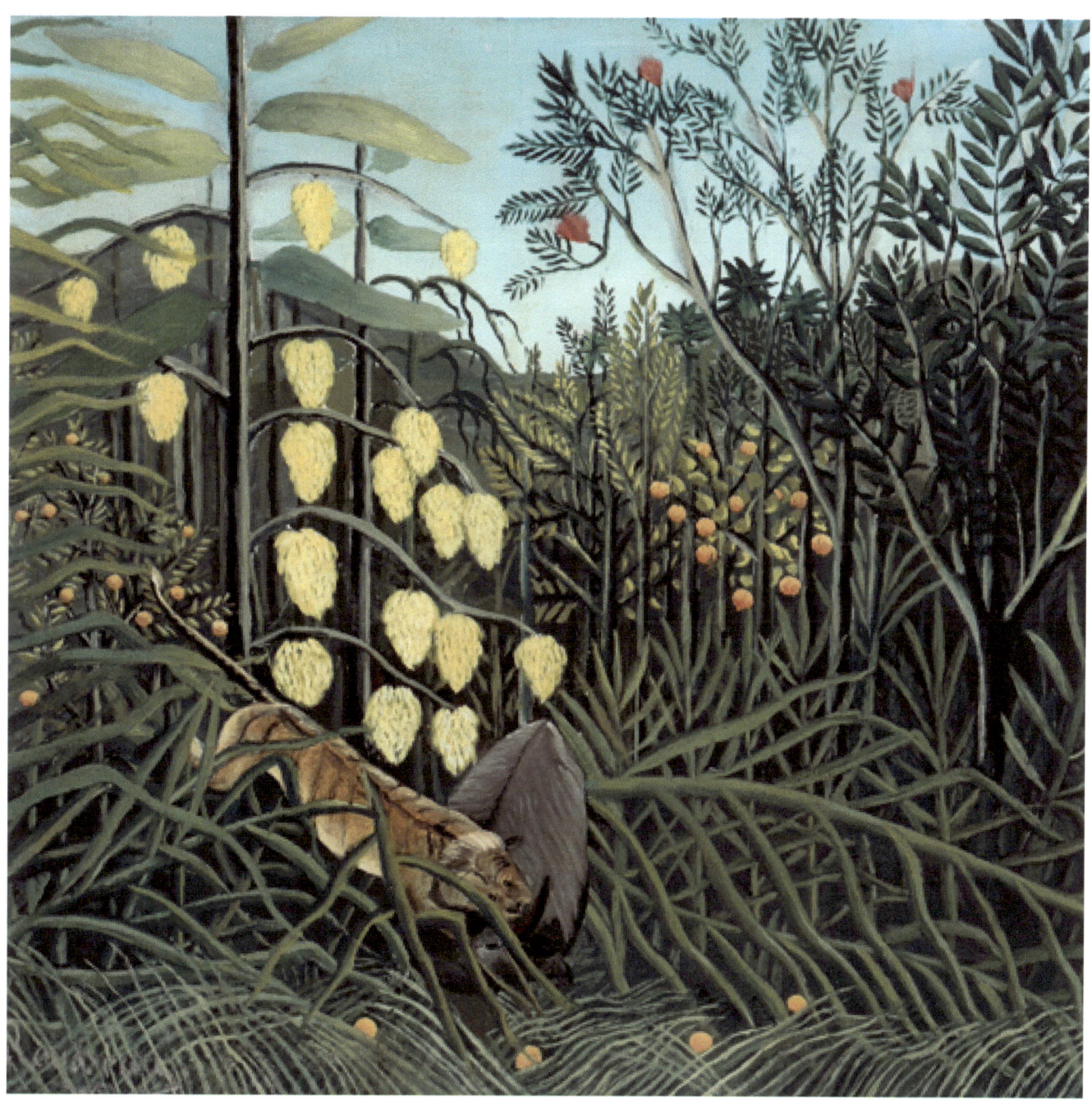

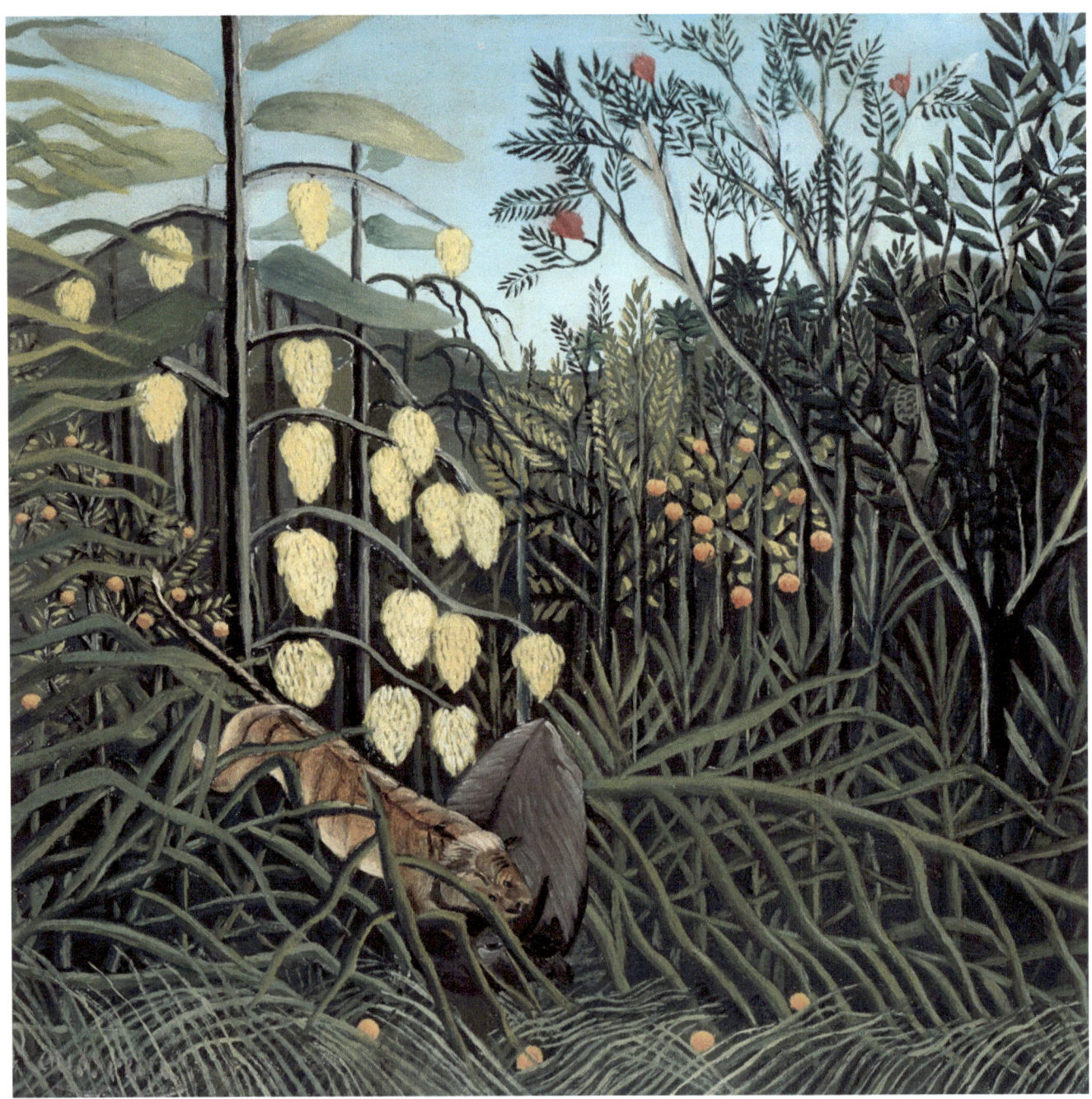

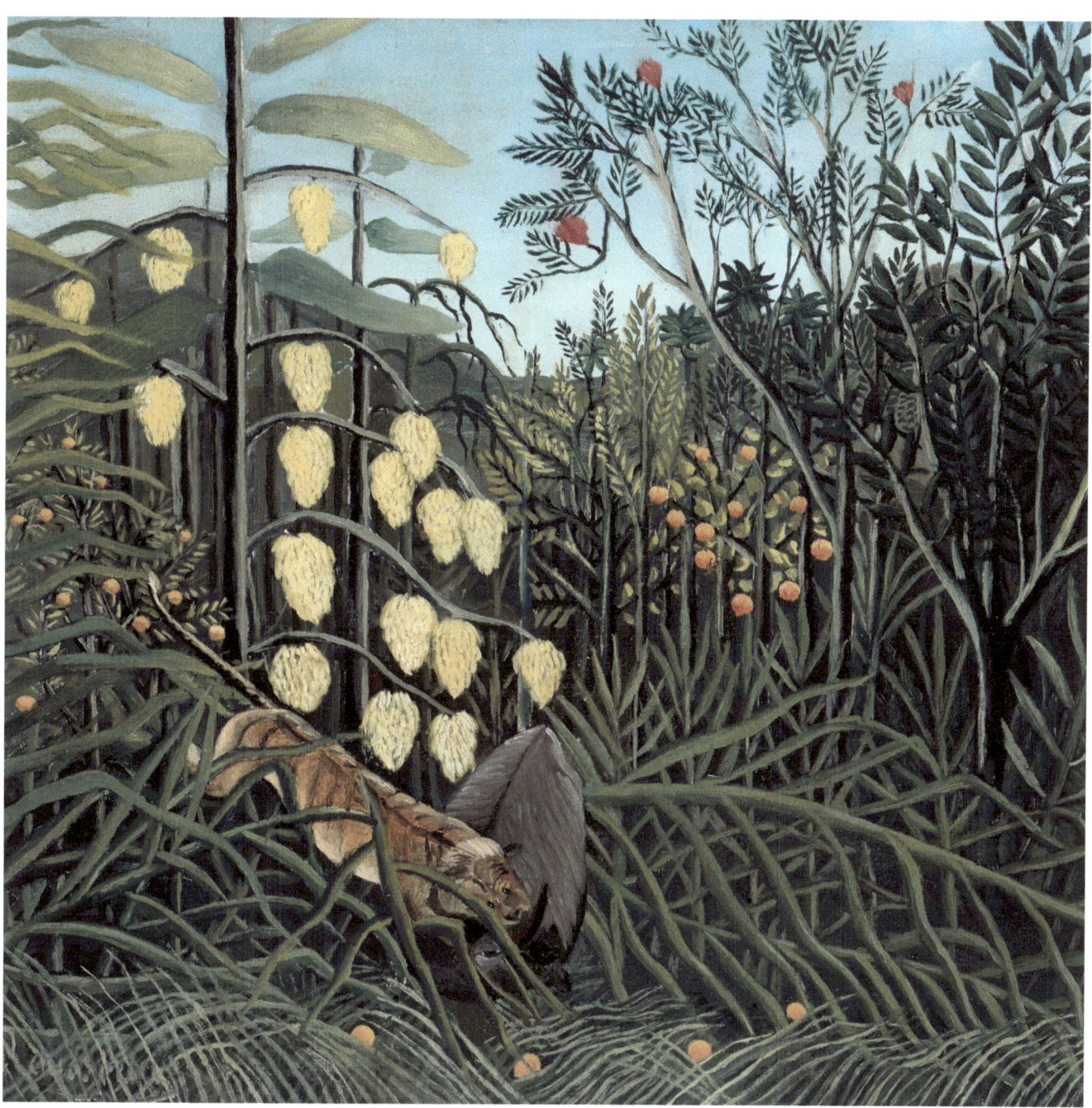

The Dream

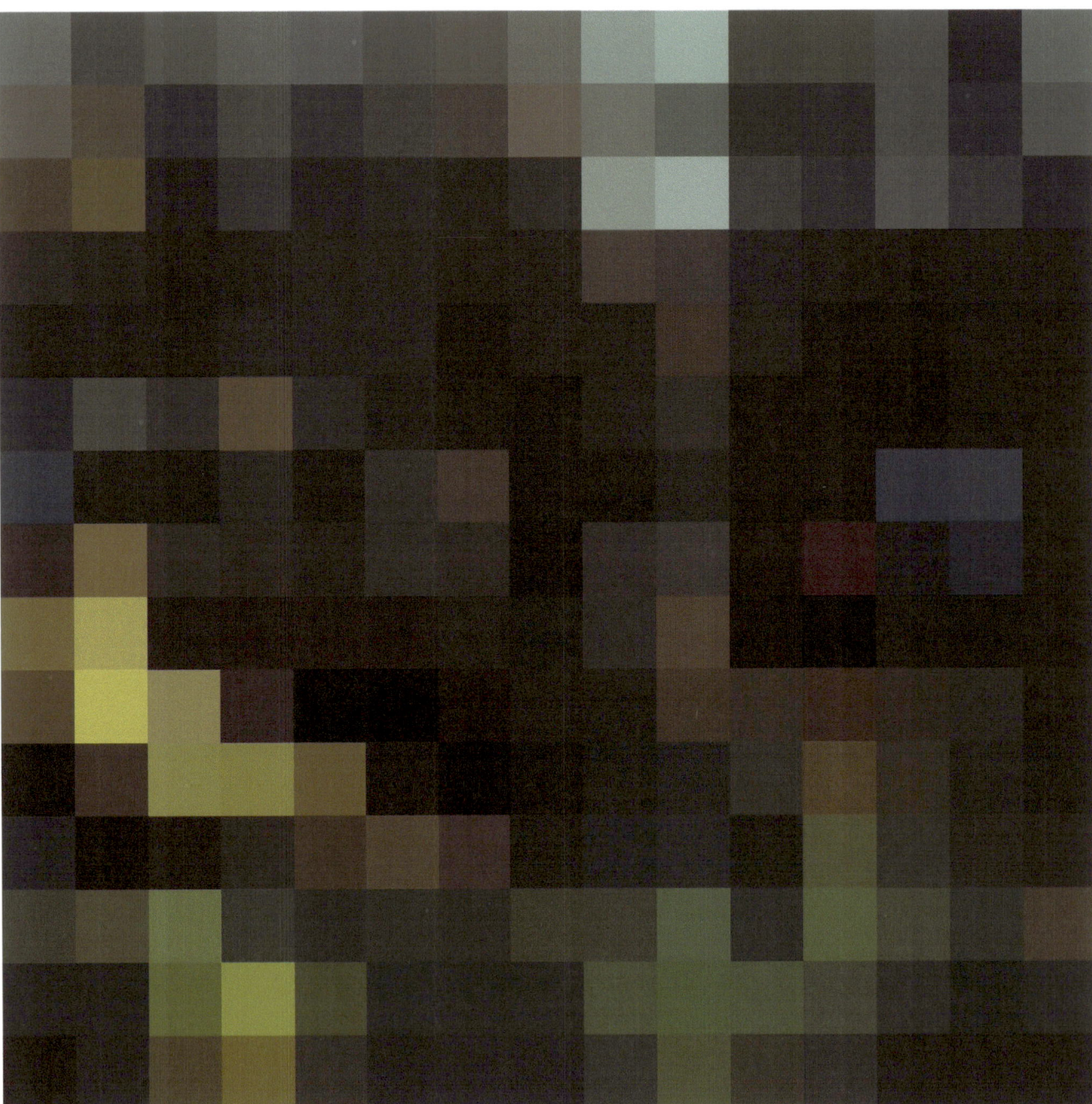

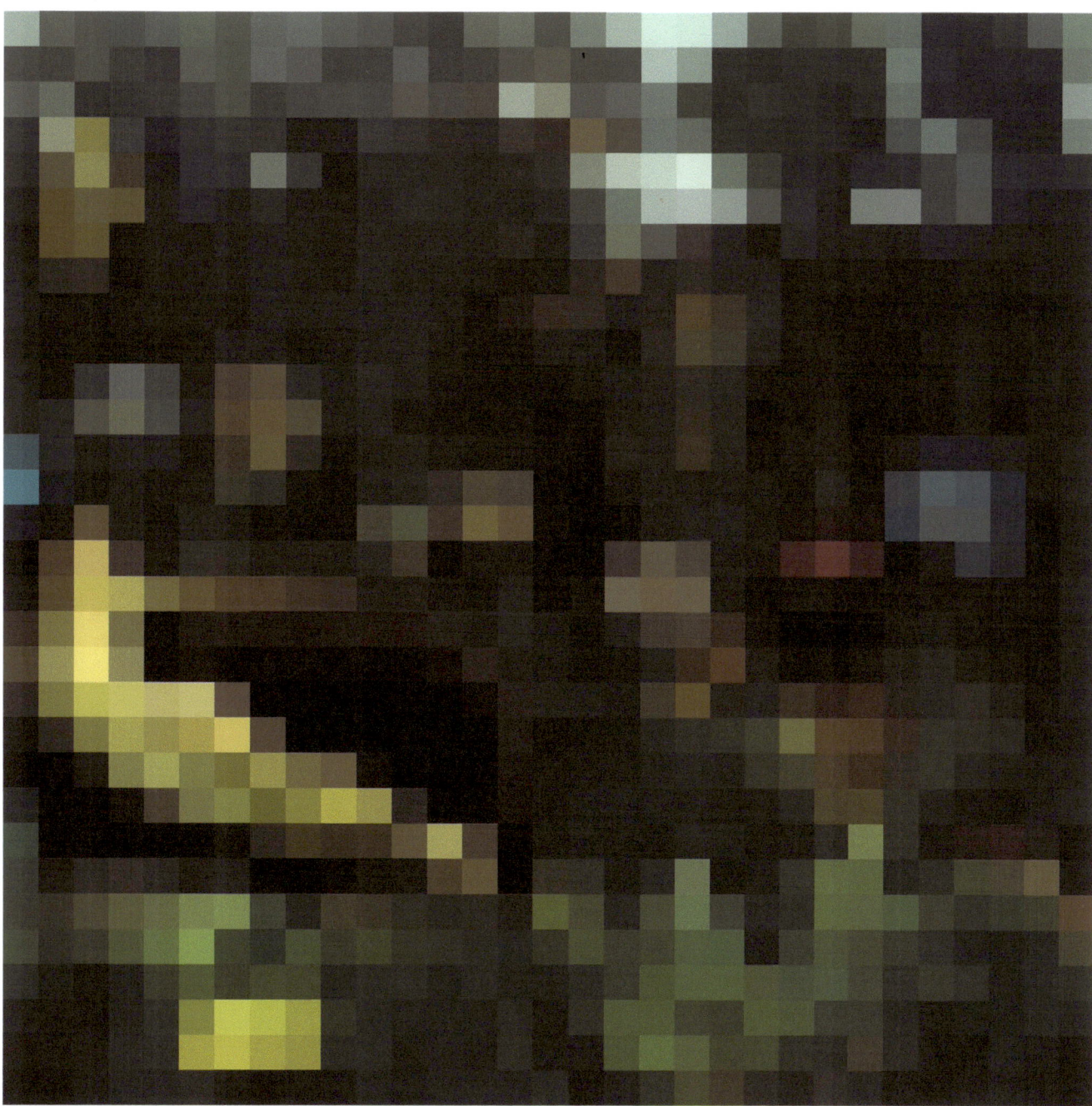

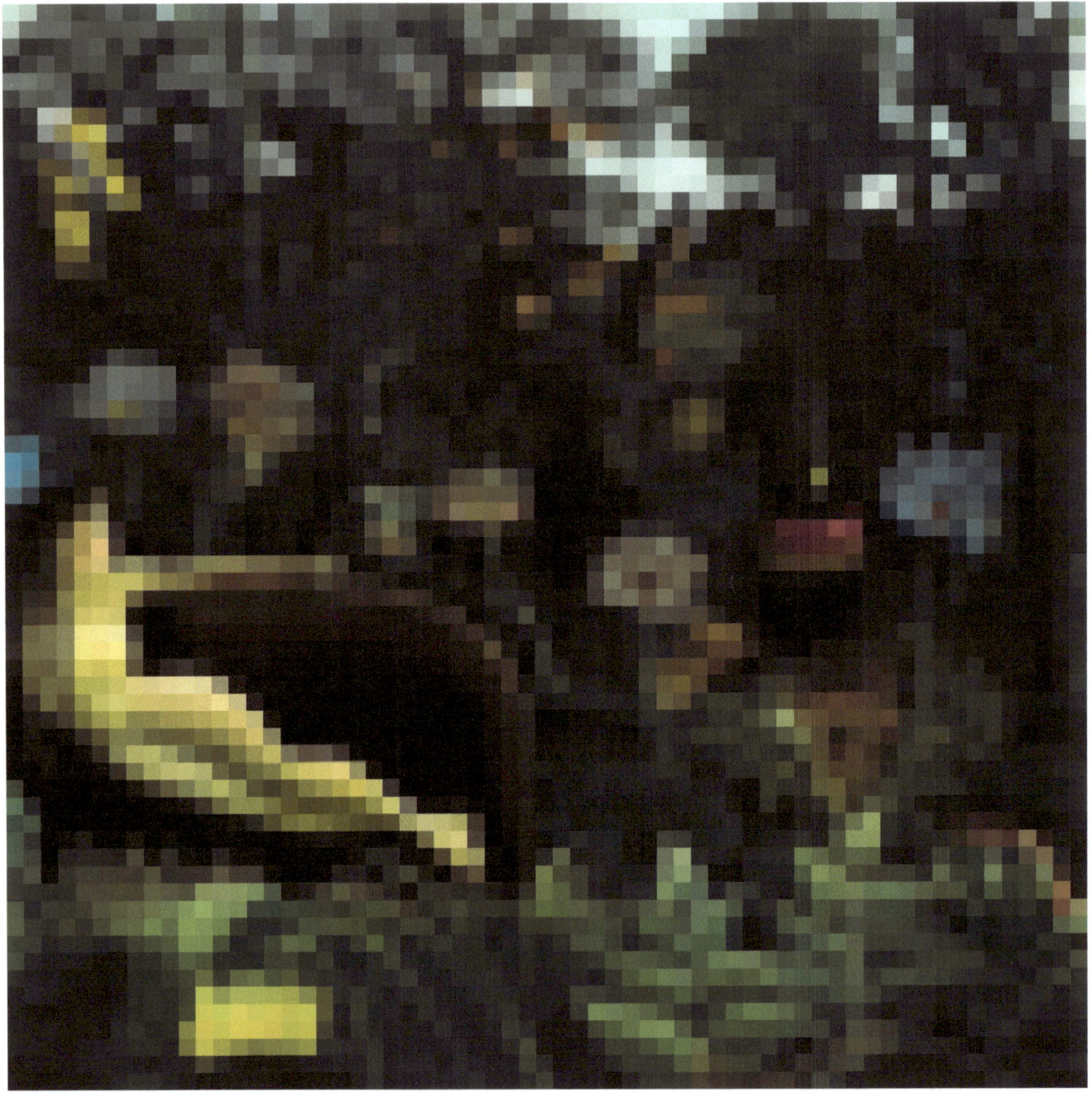

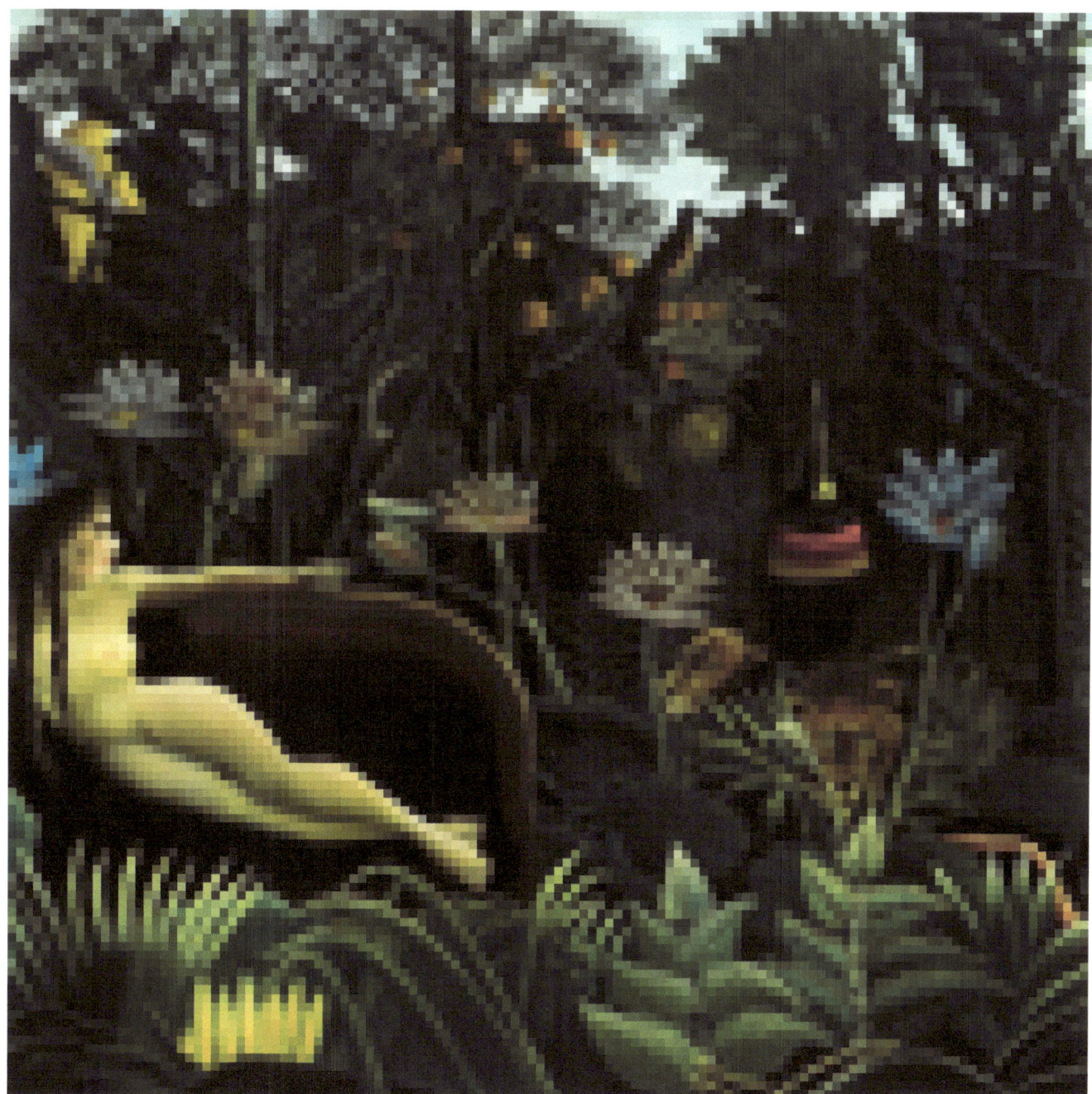

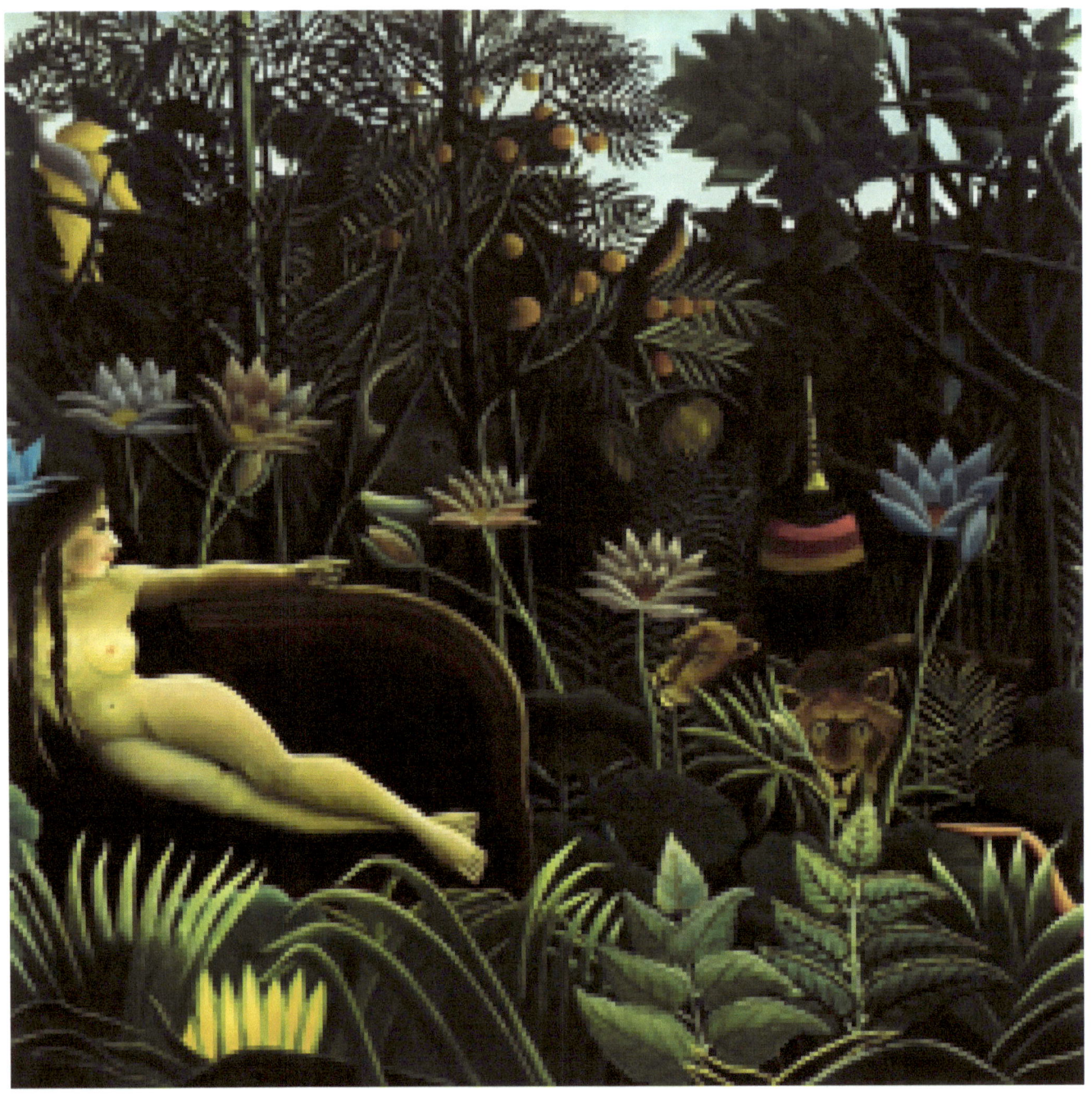

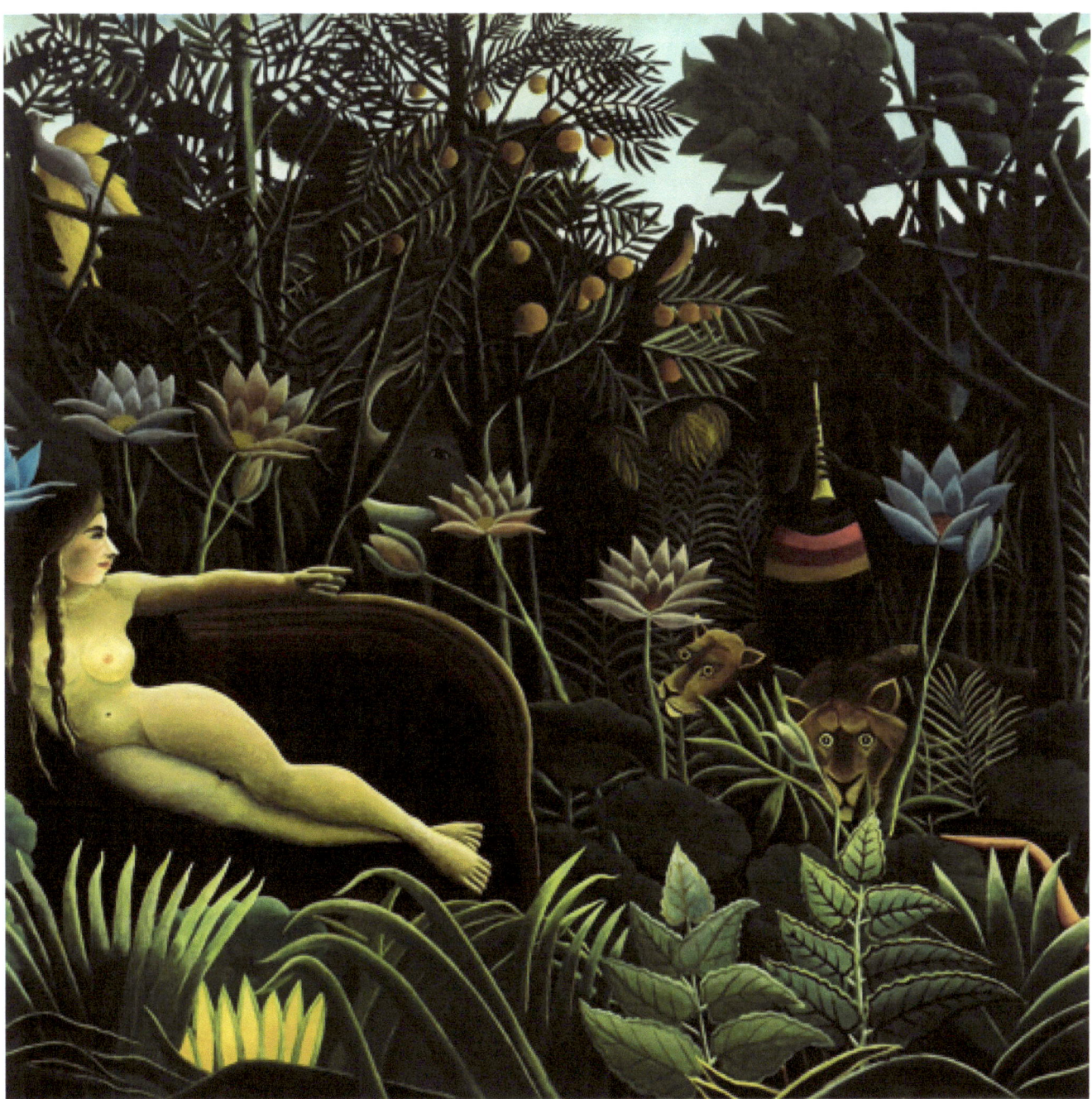

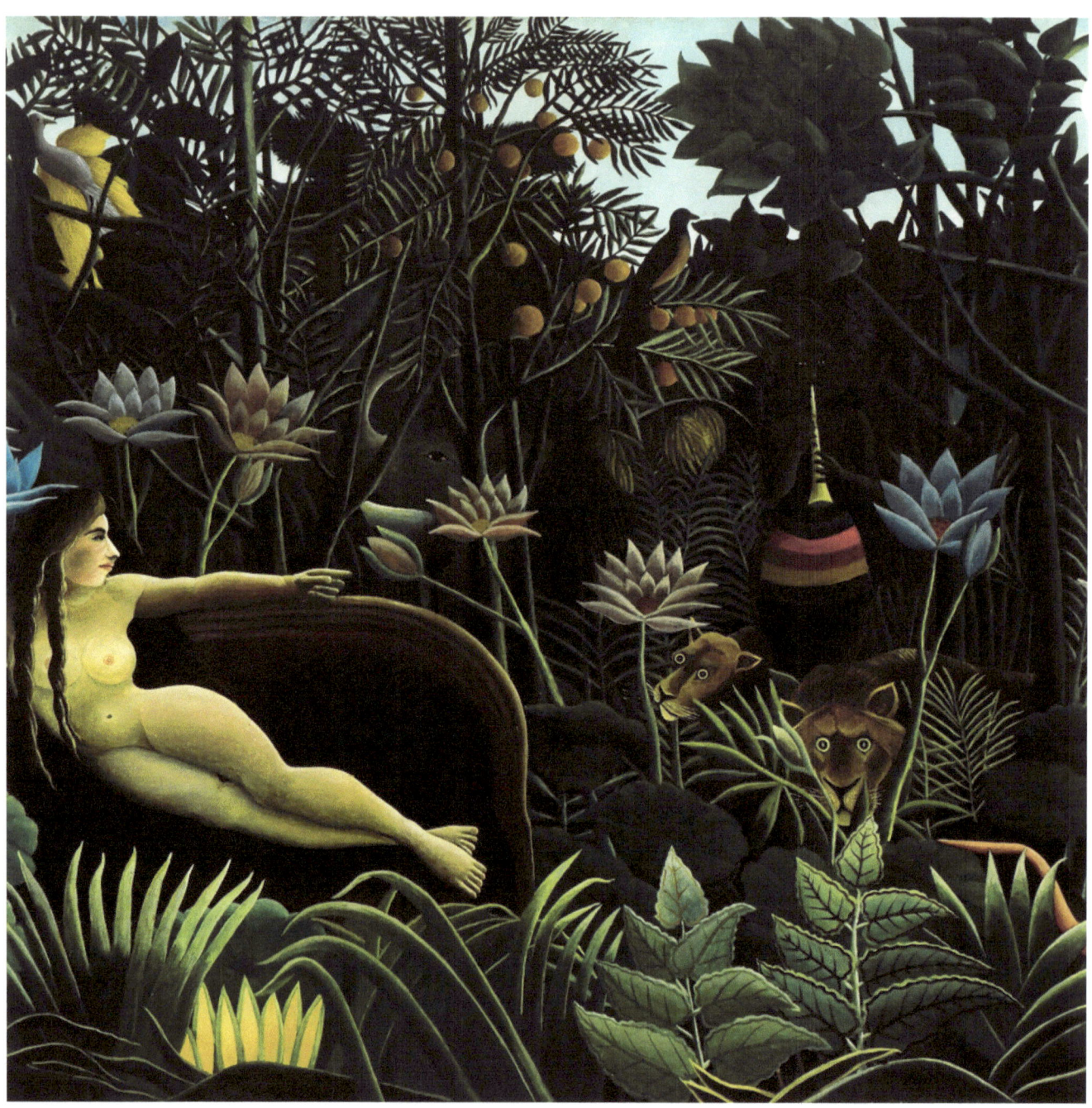

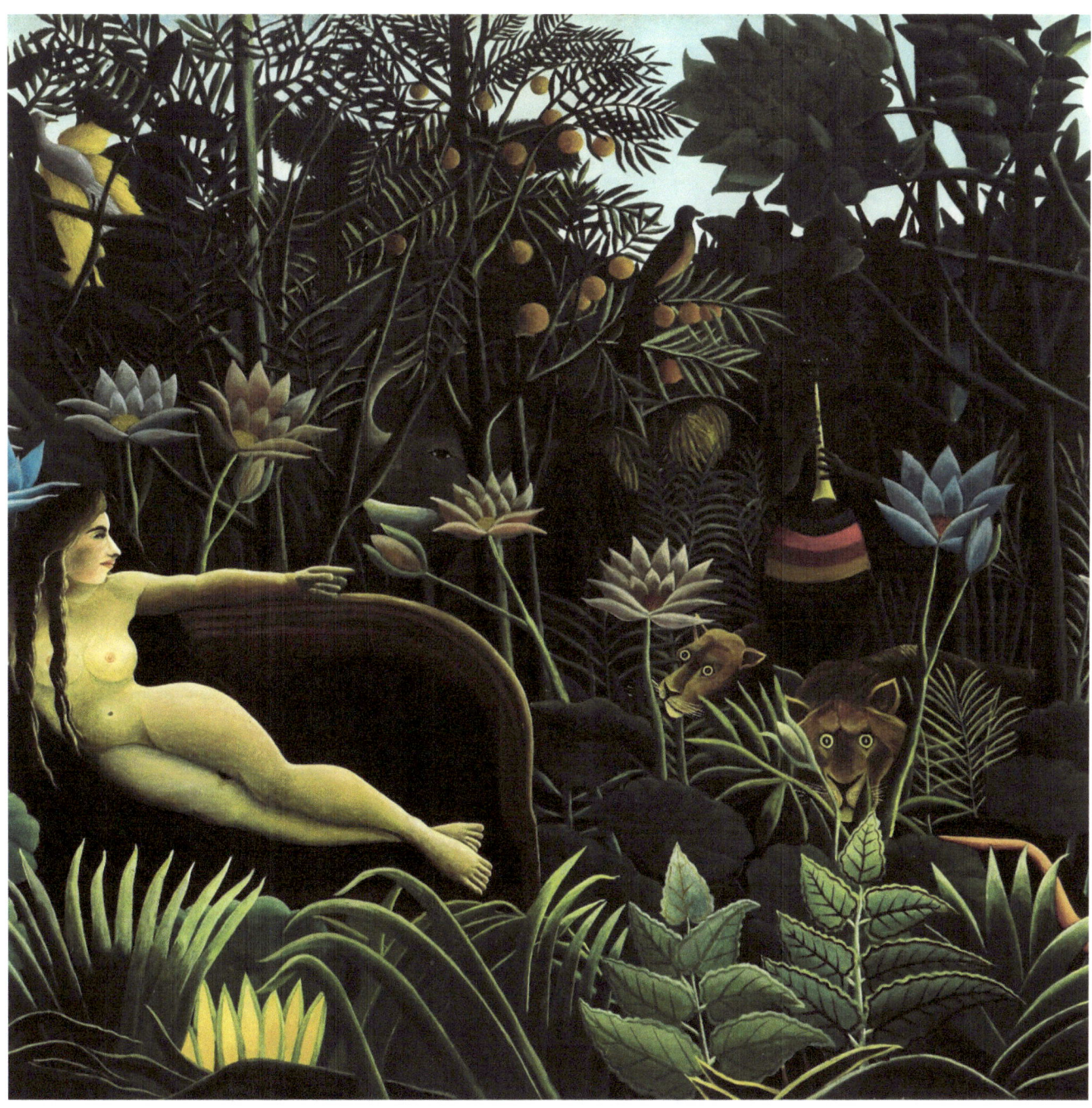

The Hungry Lion Throws Itself
on the Antelope

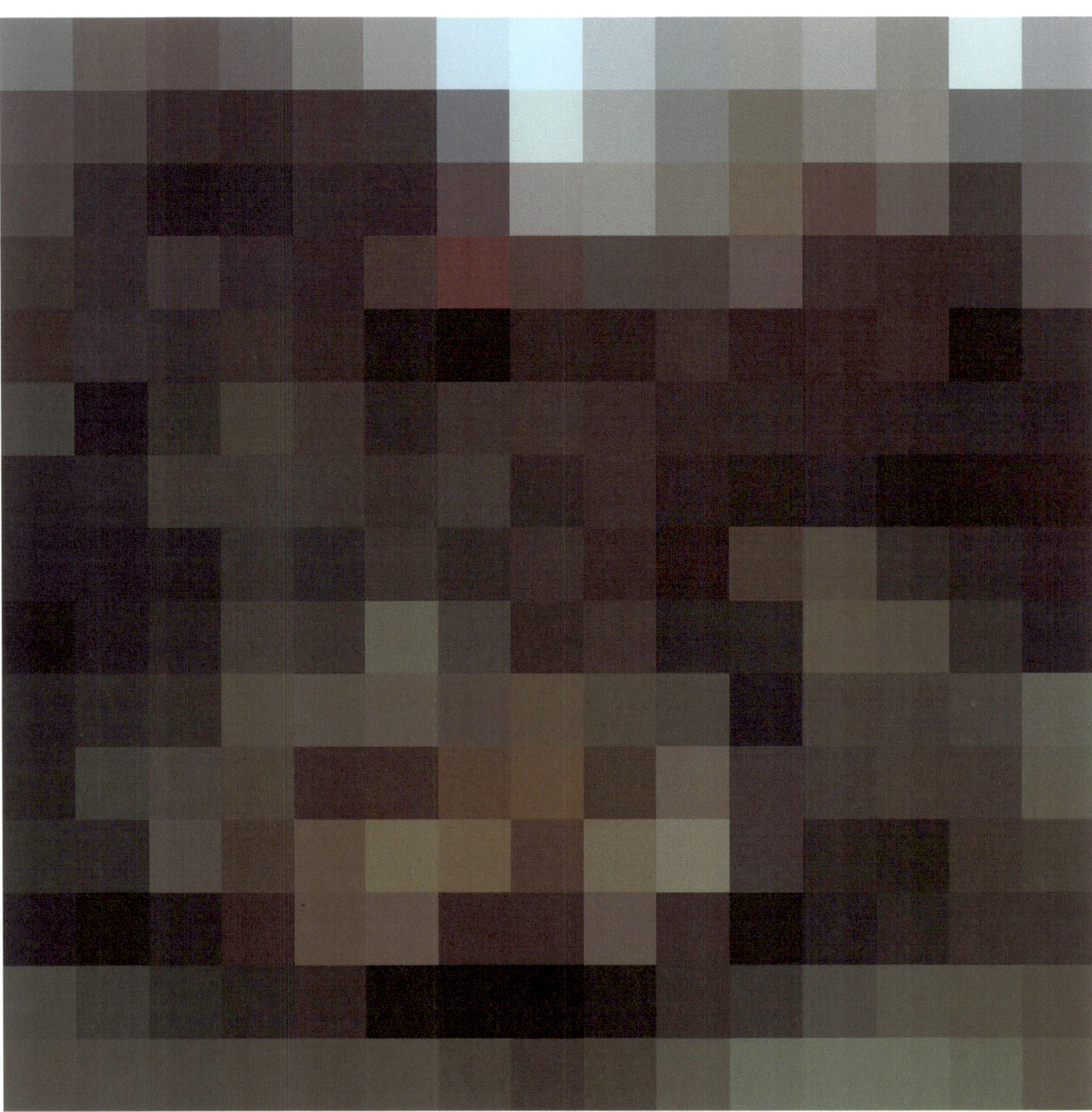

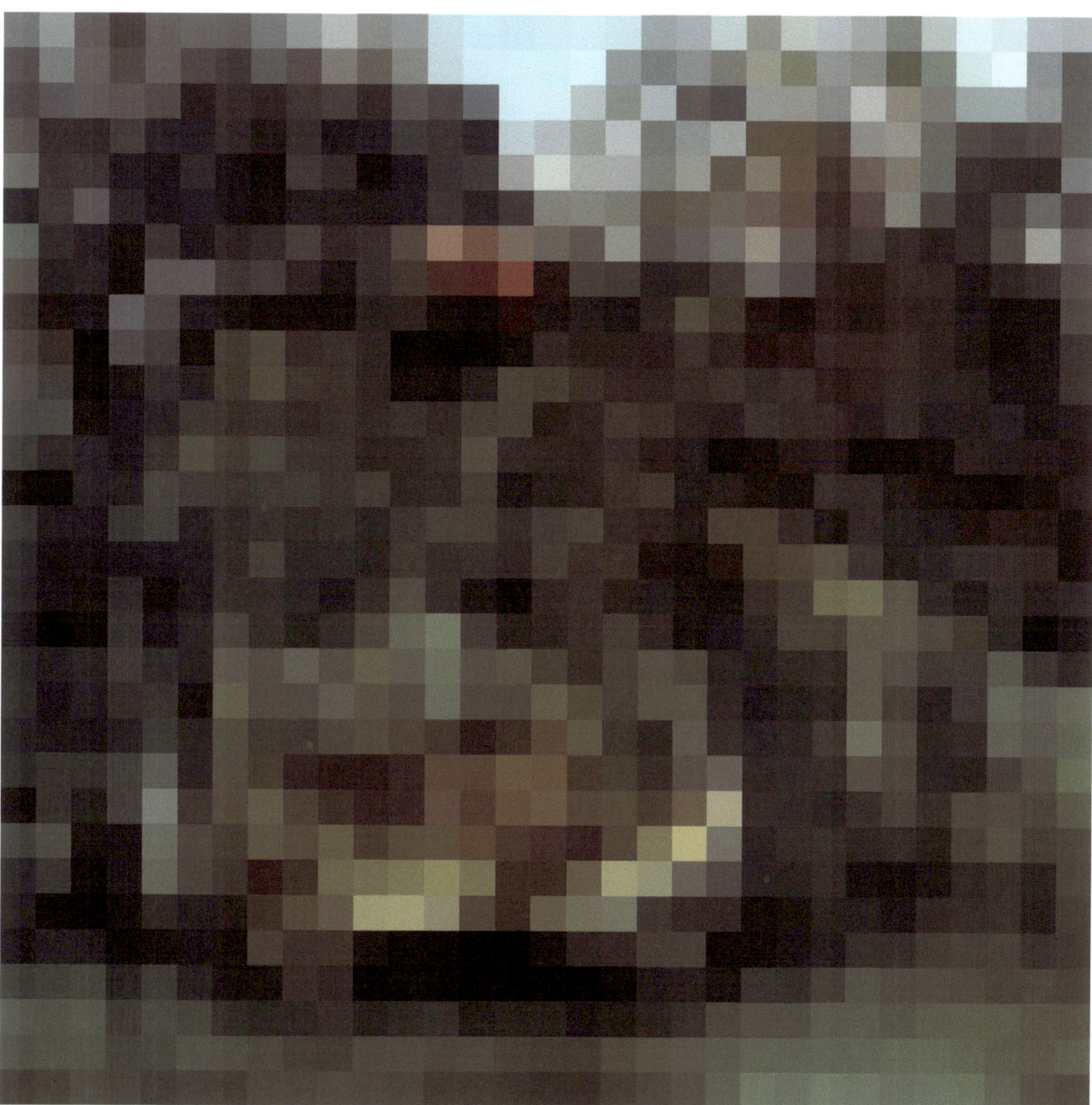

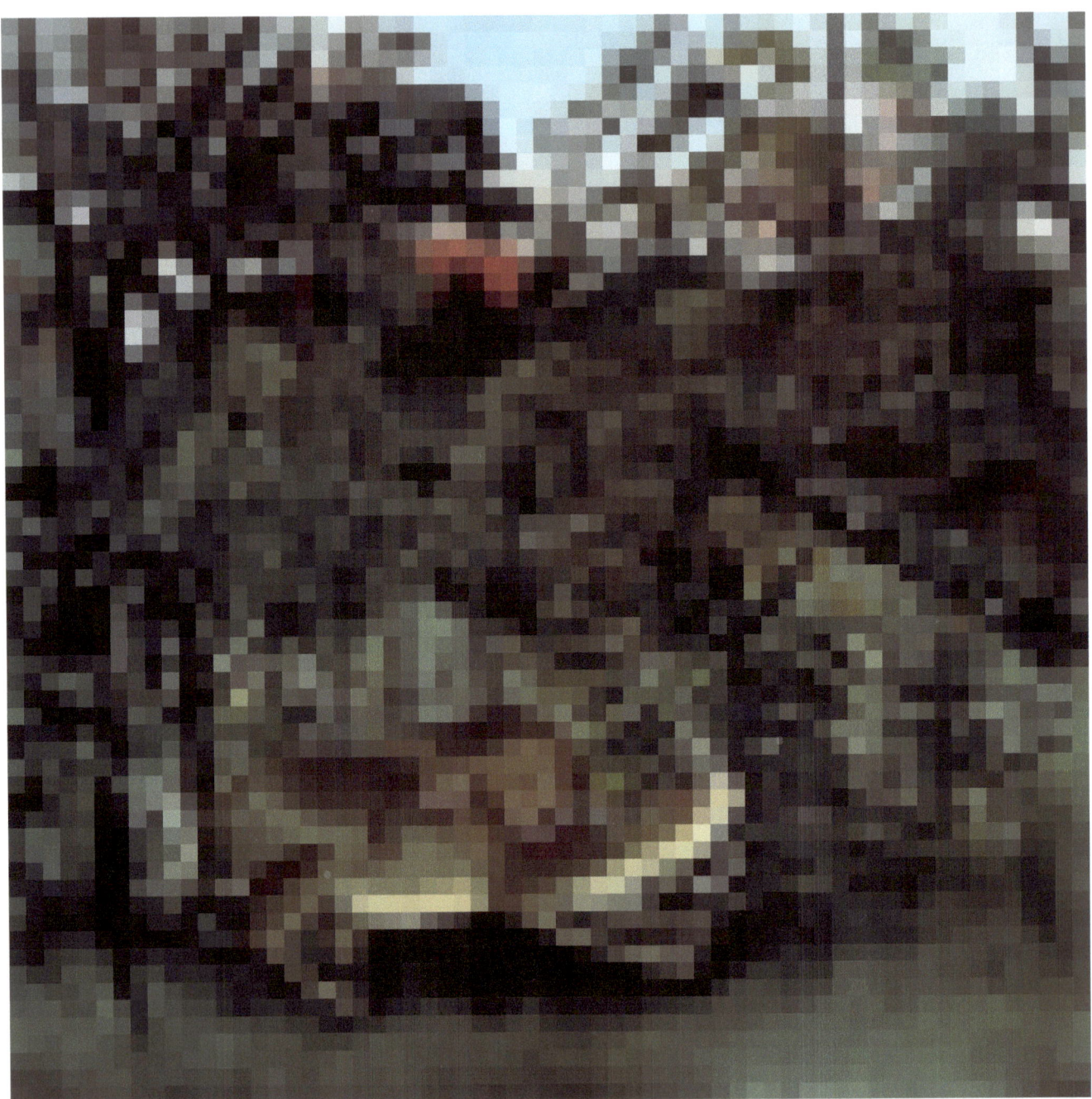

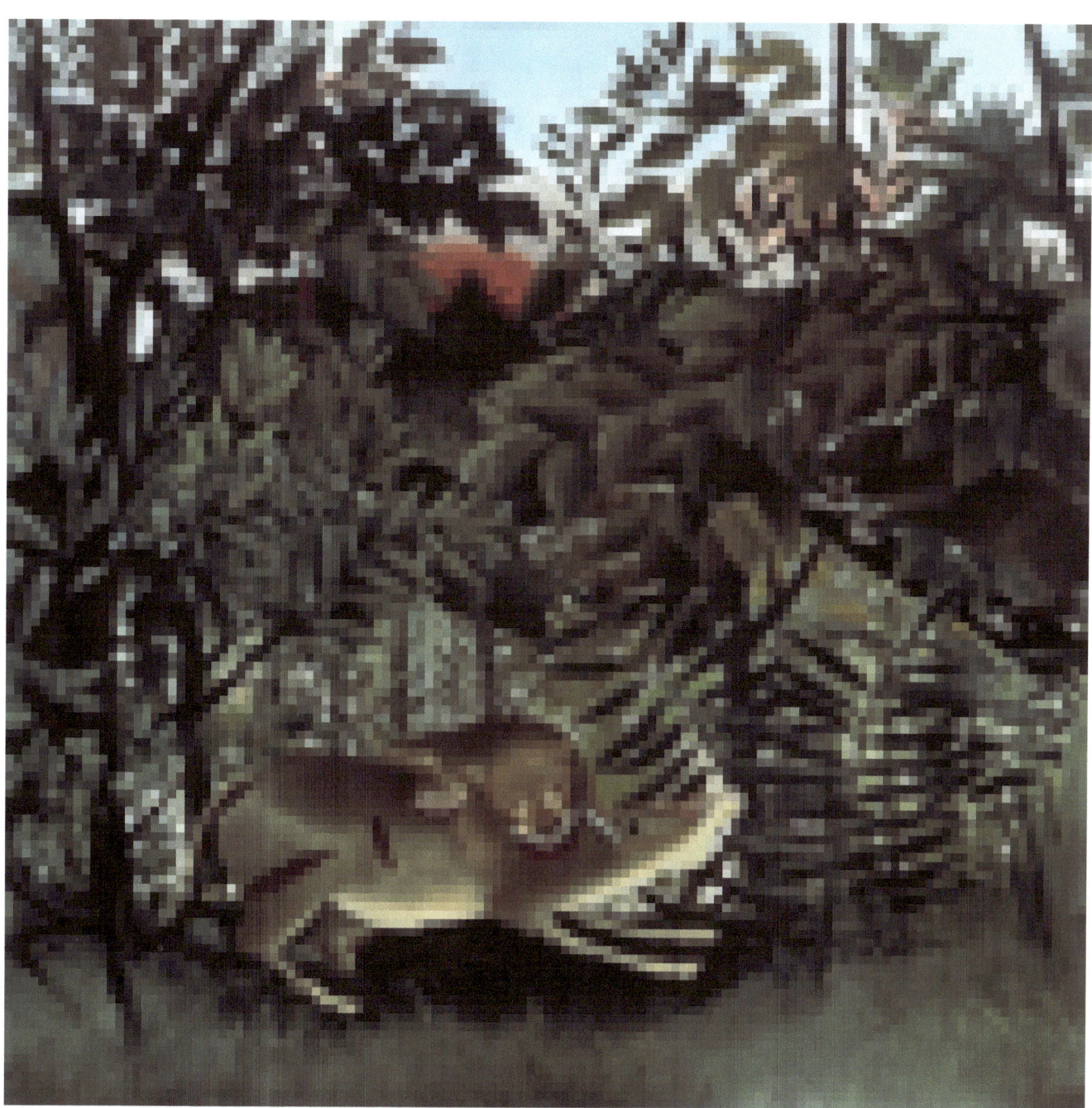

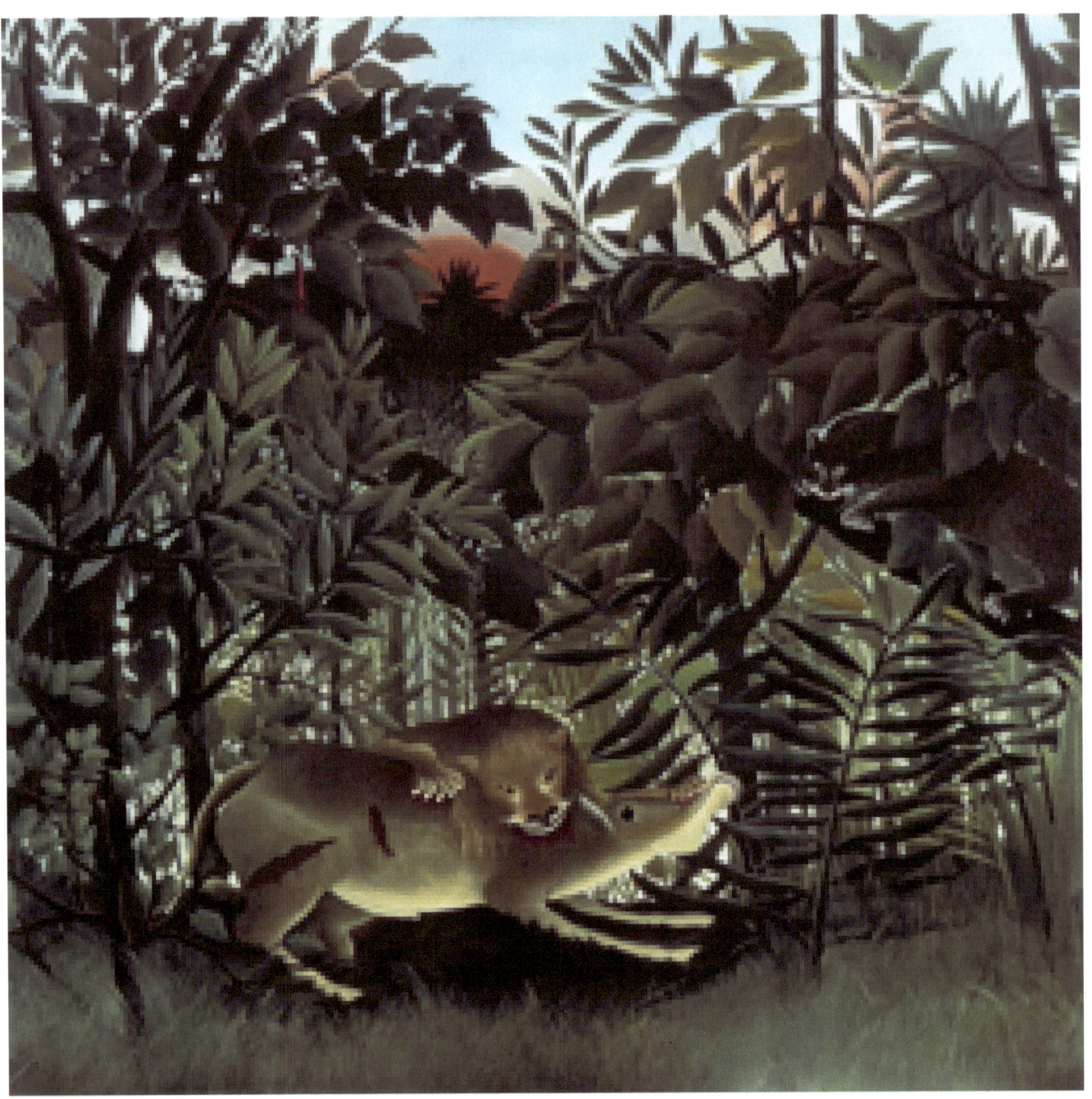

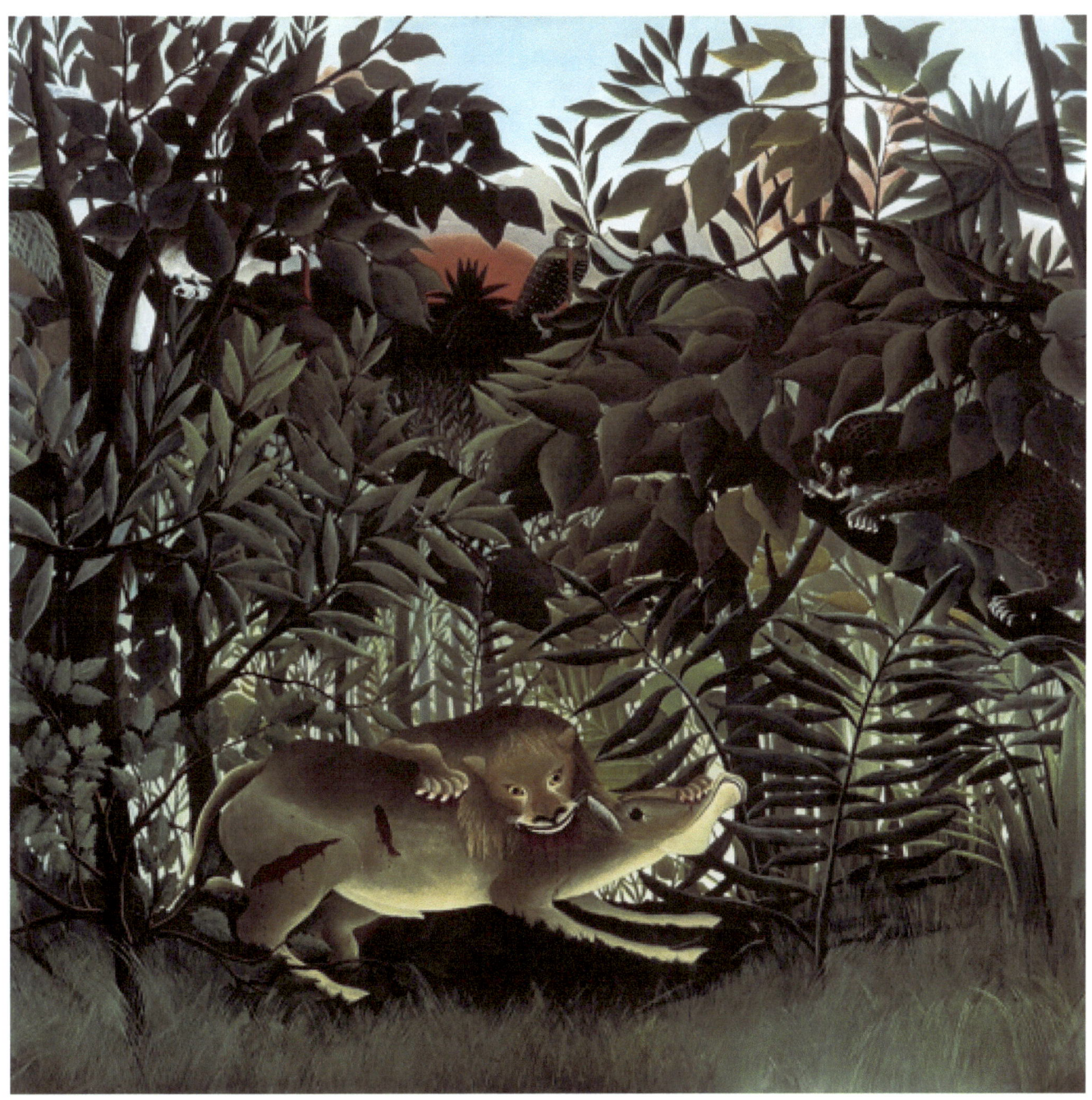

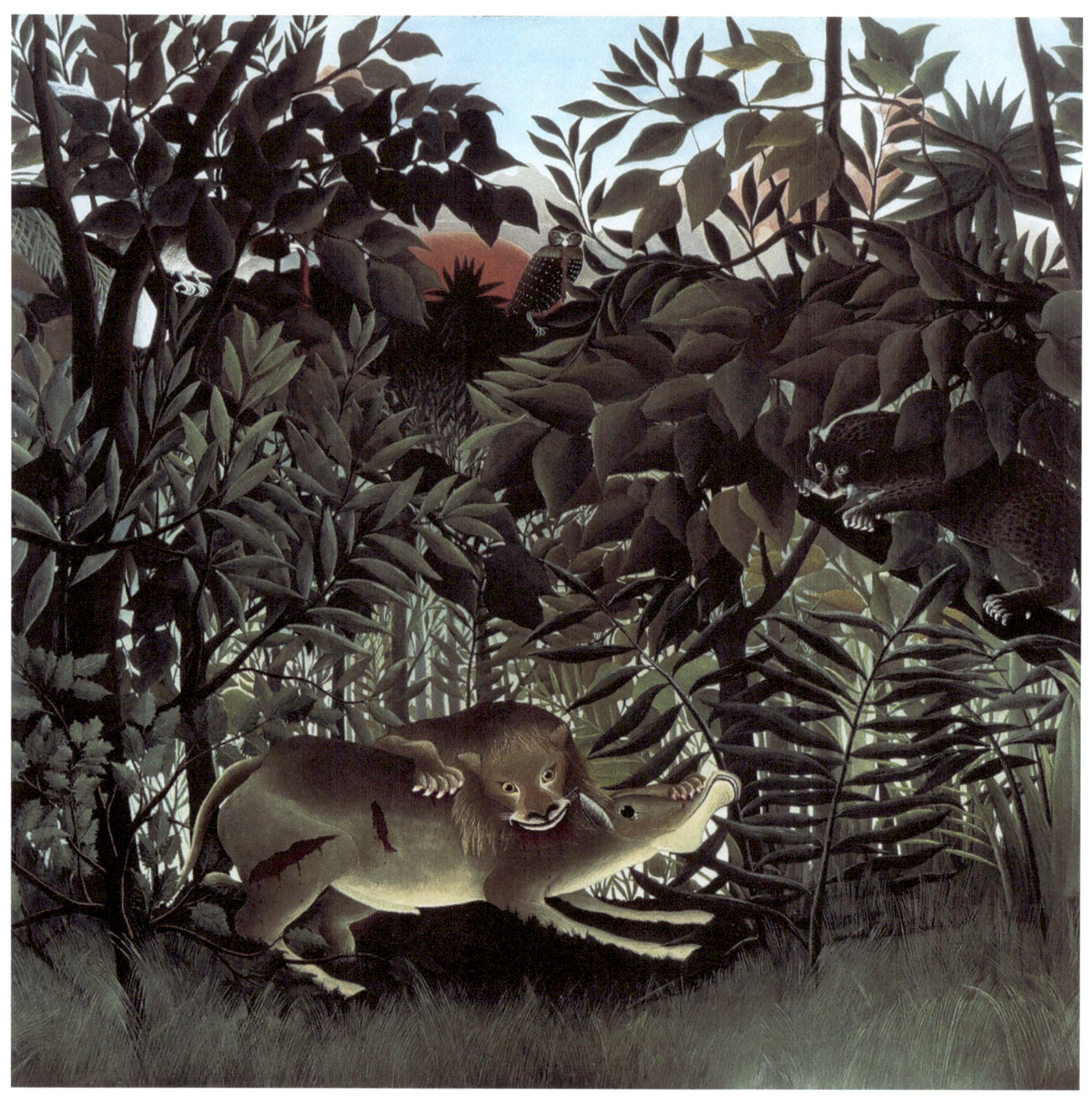

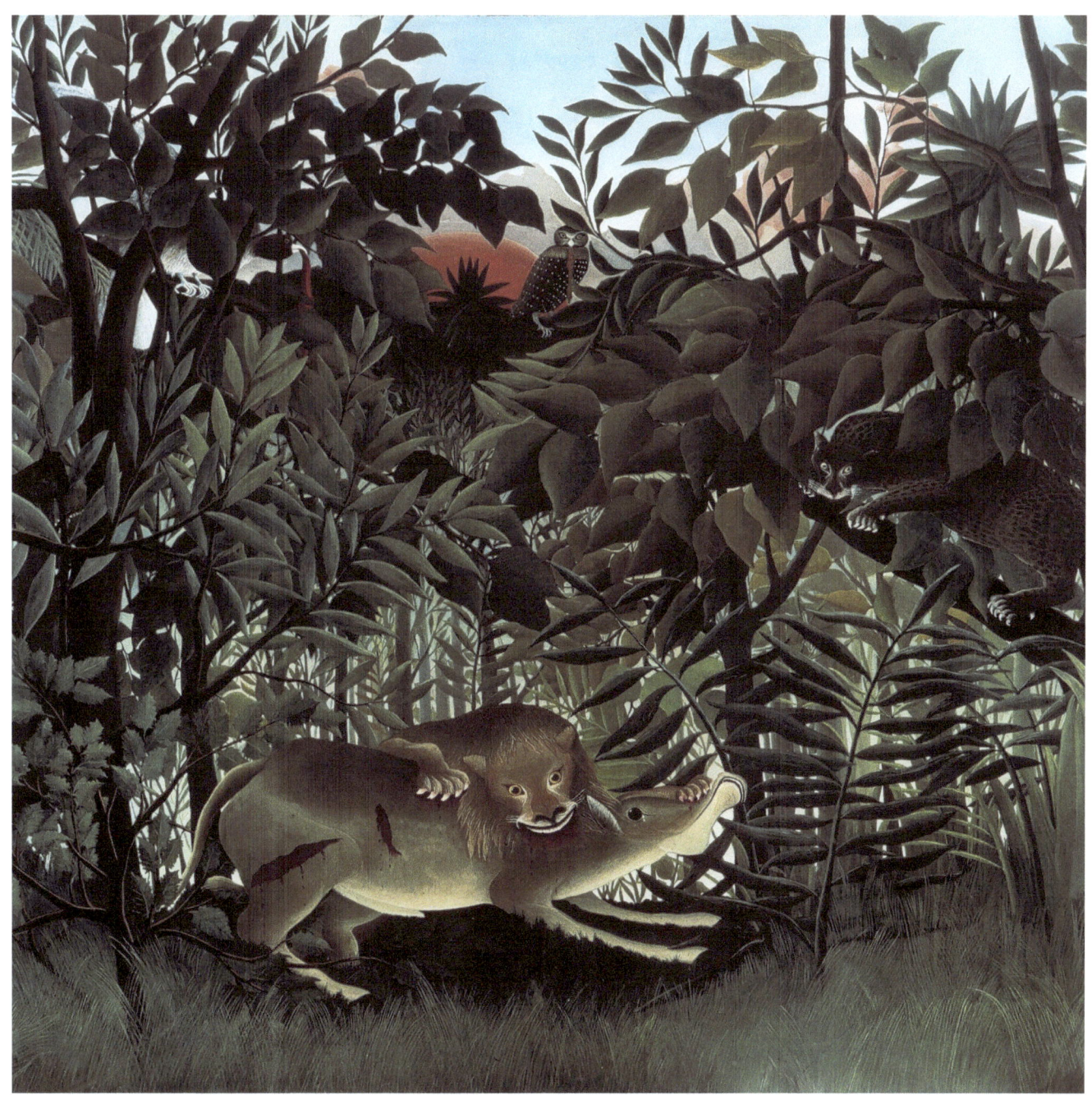

The Representatives of Foreign
Powers Coming to Greet the
Republic as a Sign of Peace

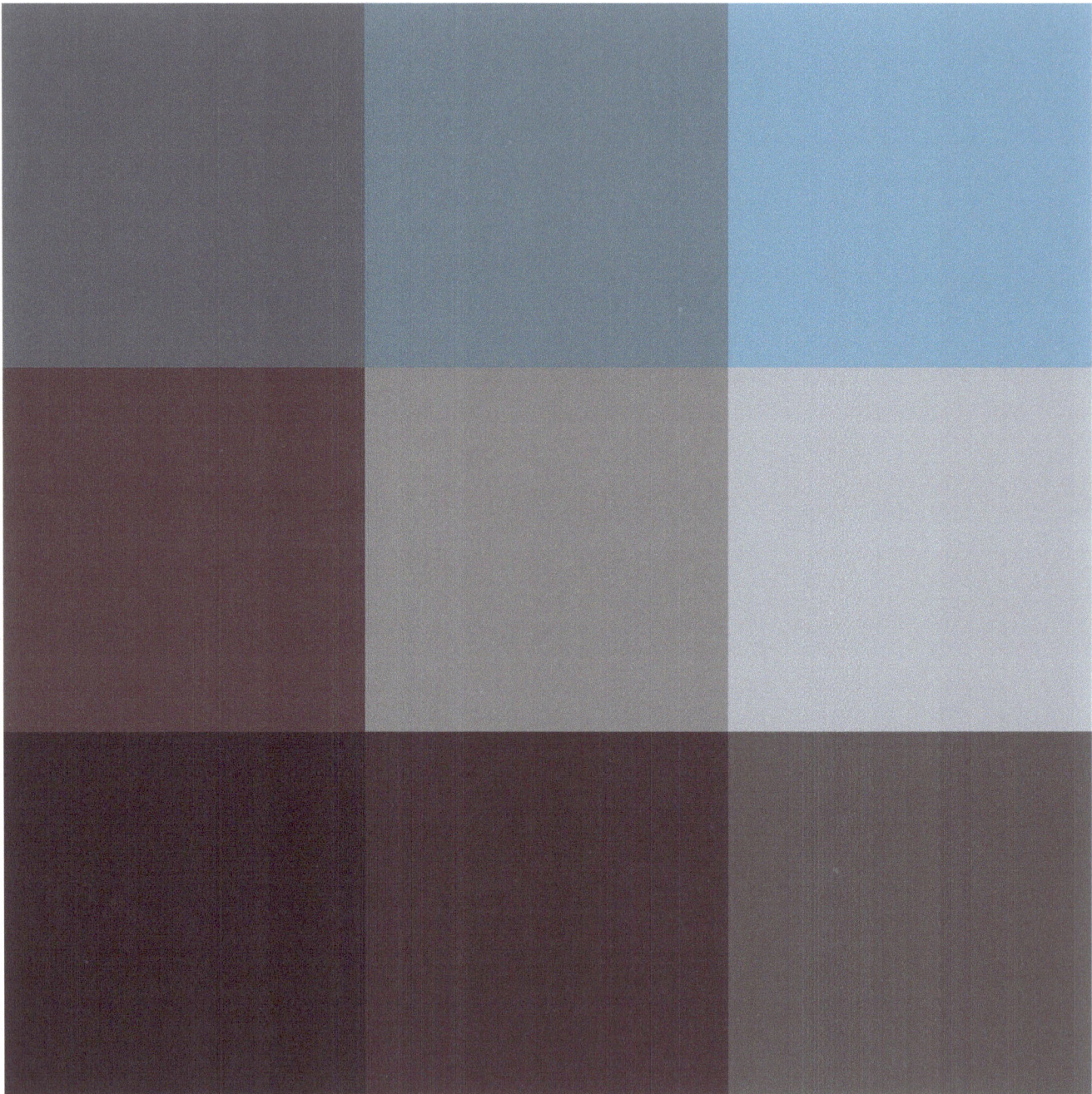

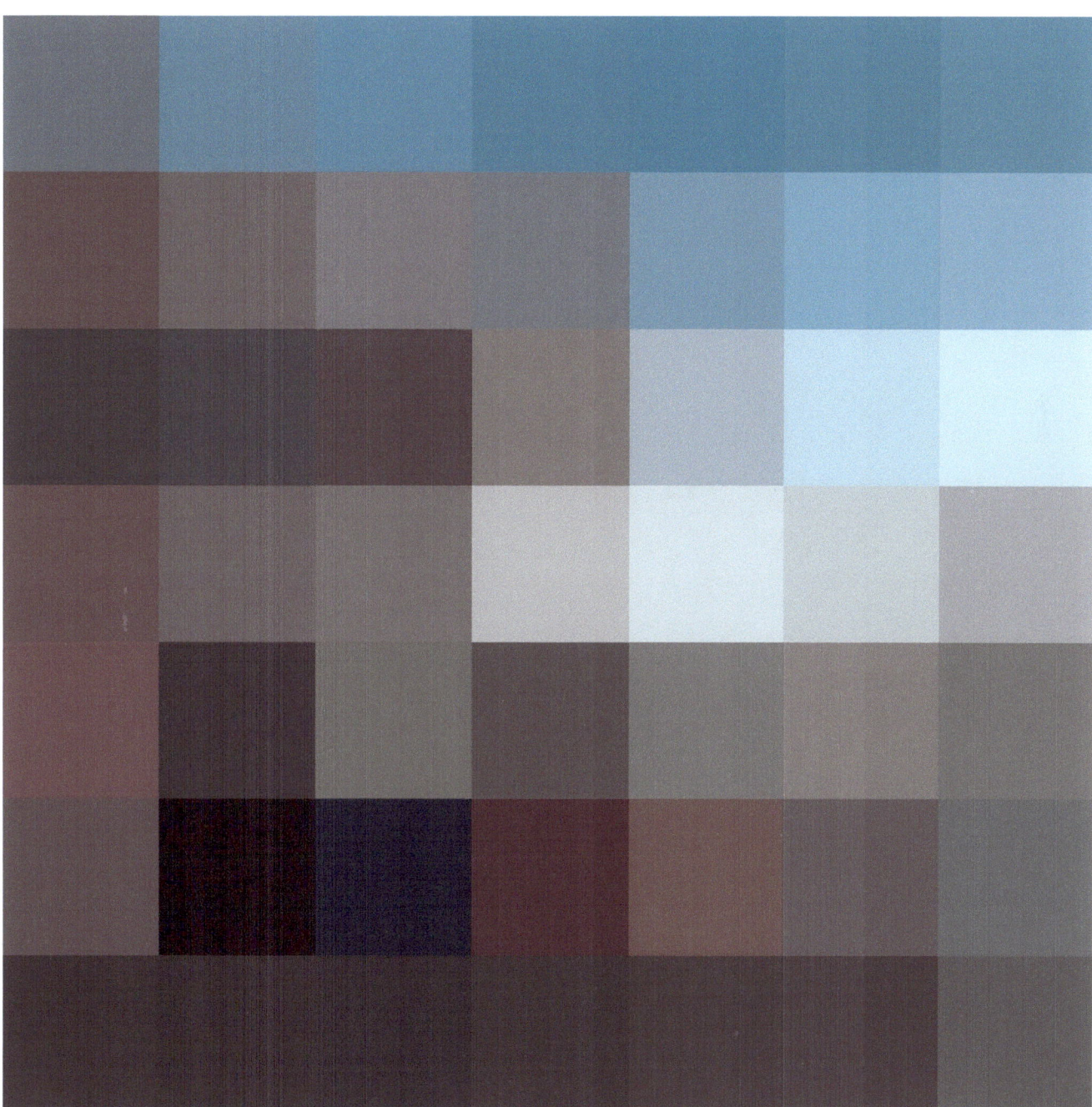

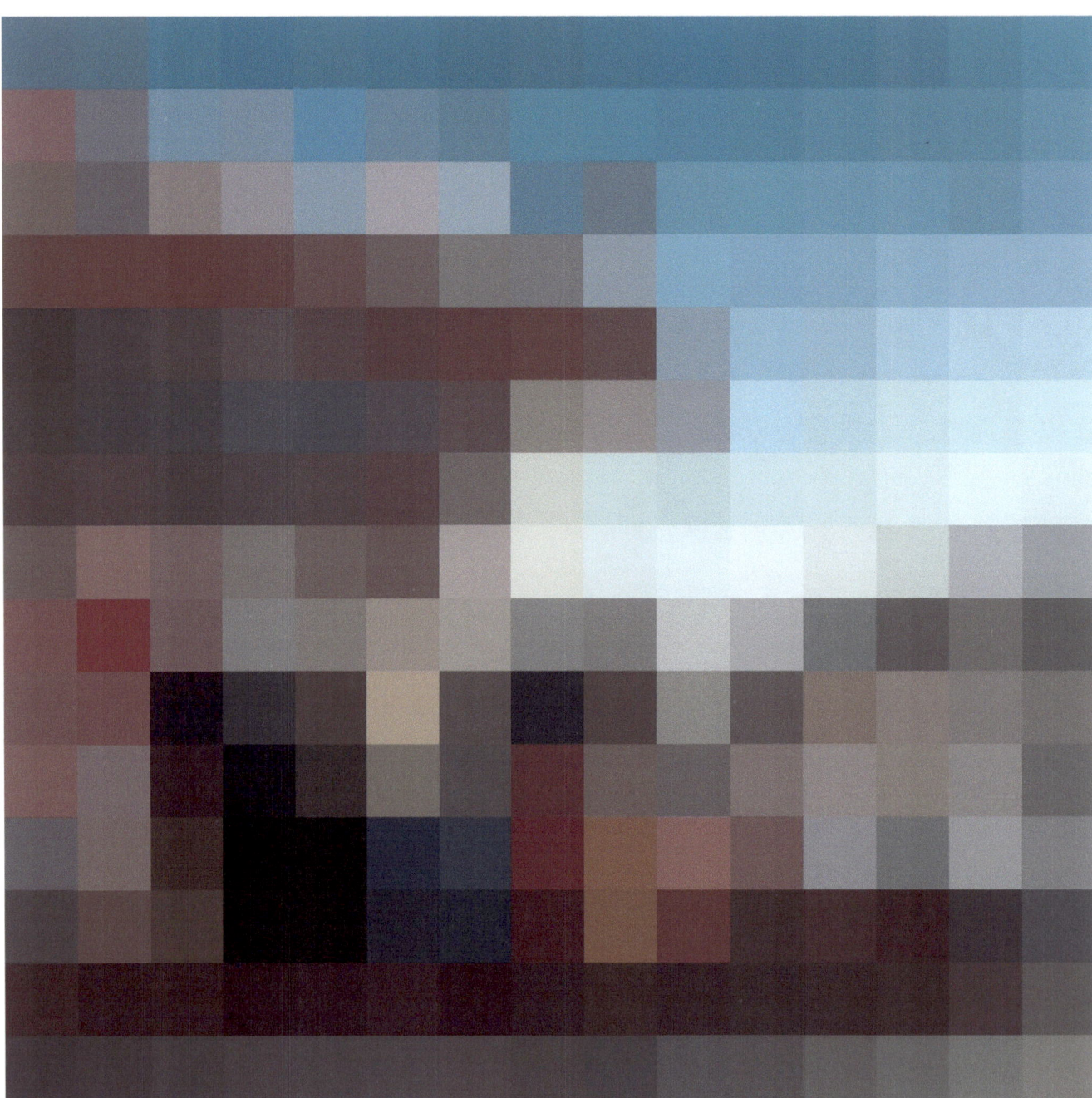

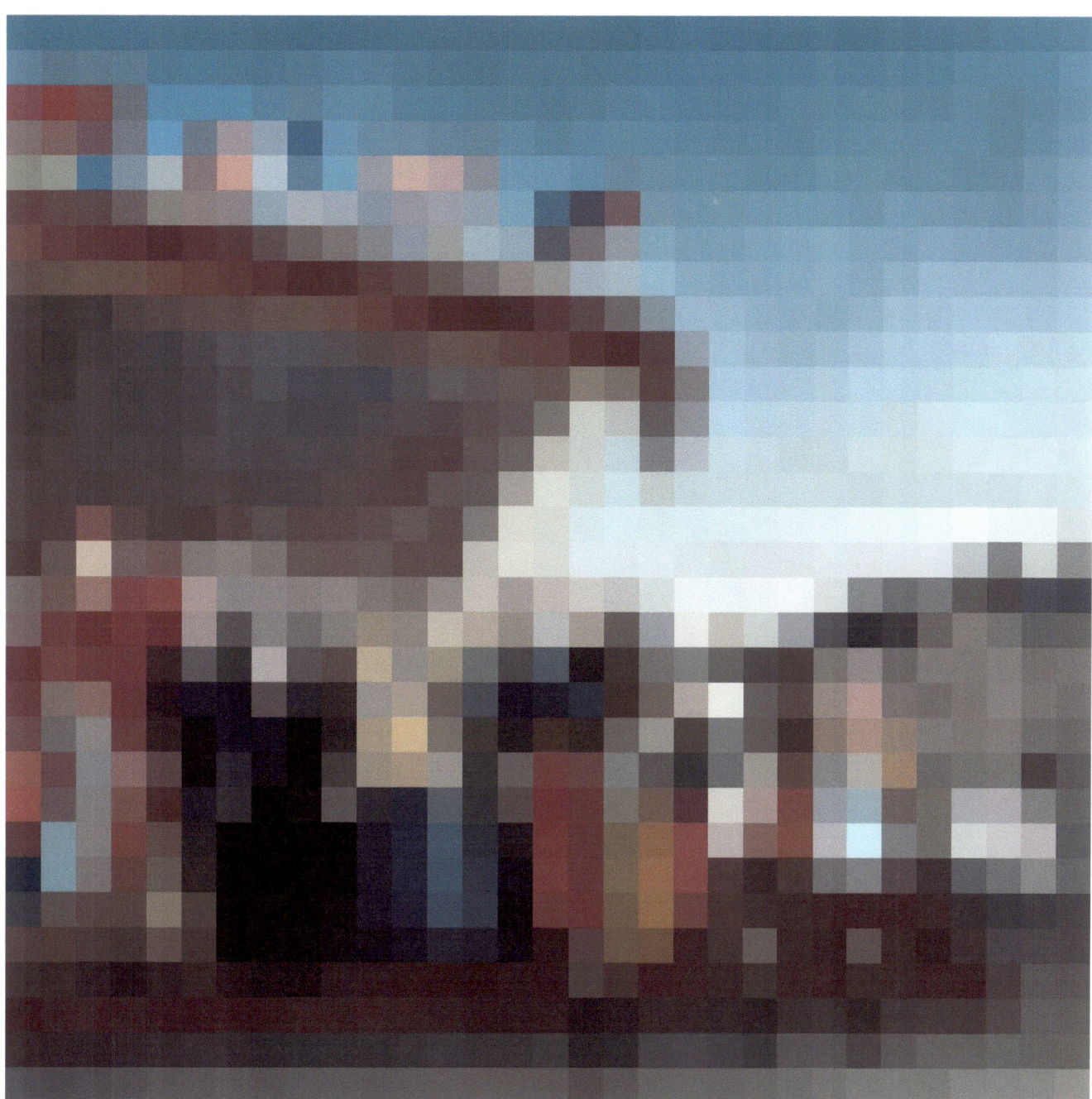

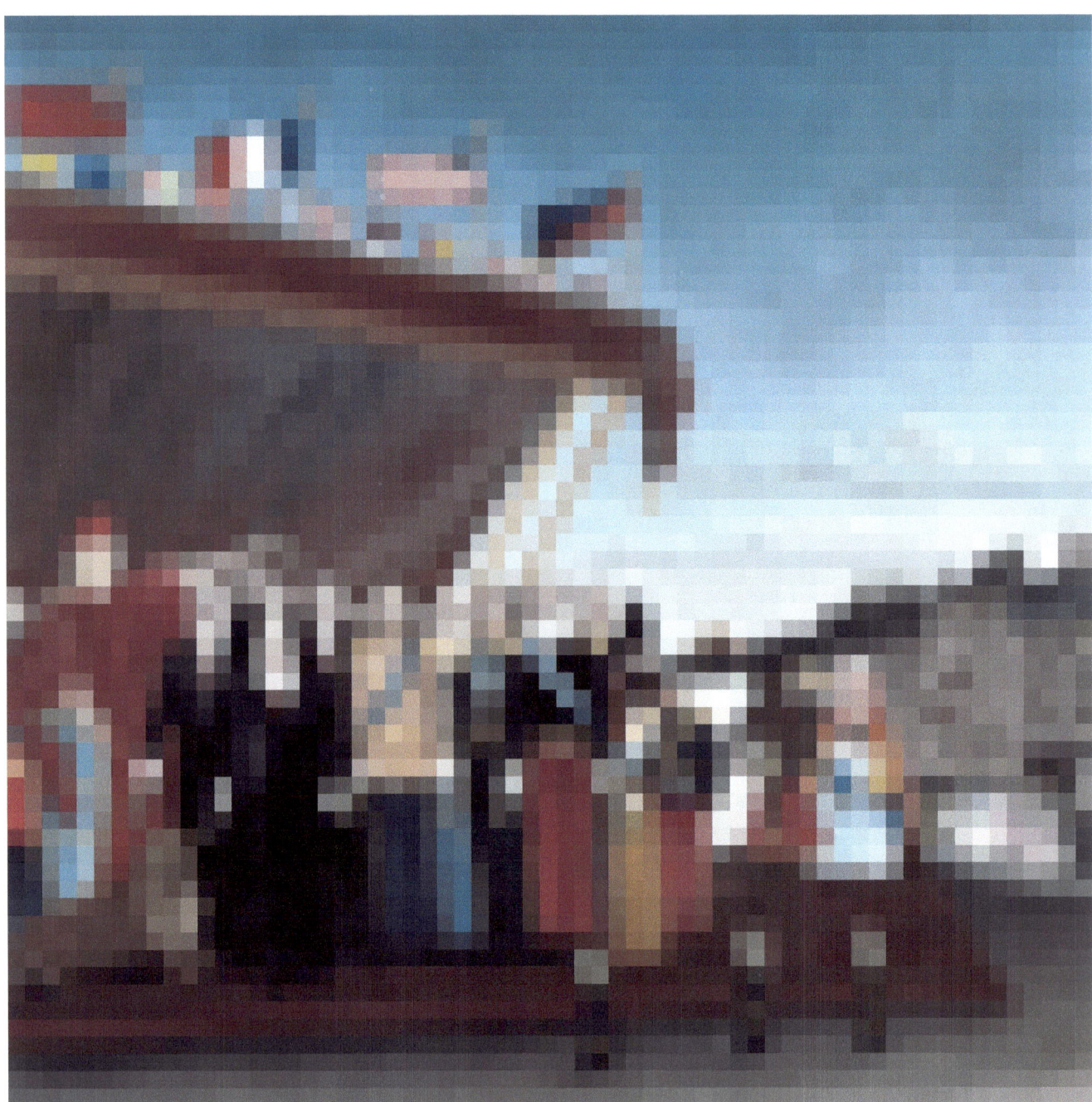

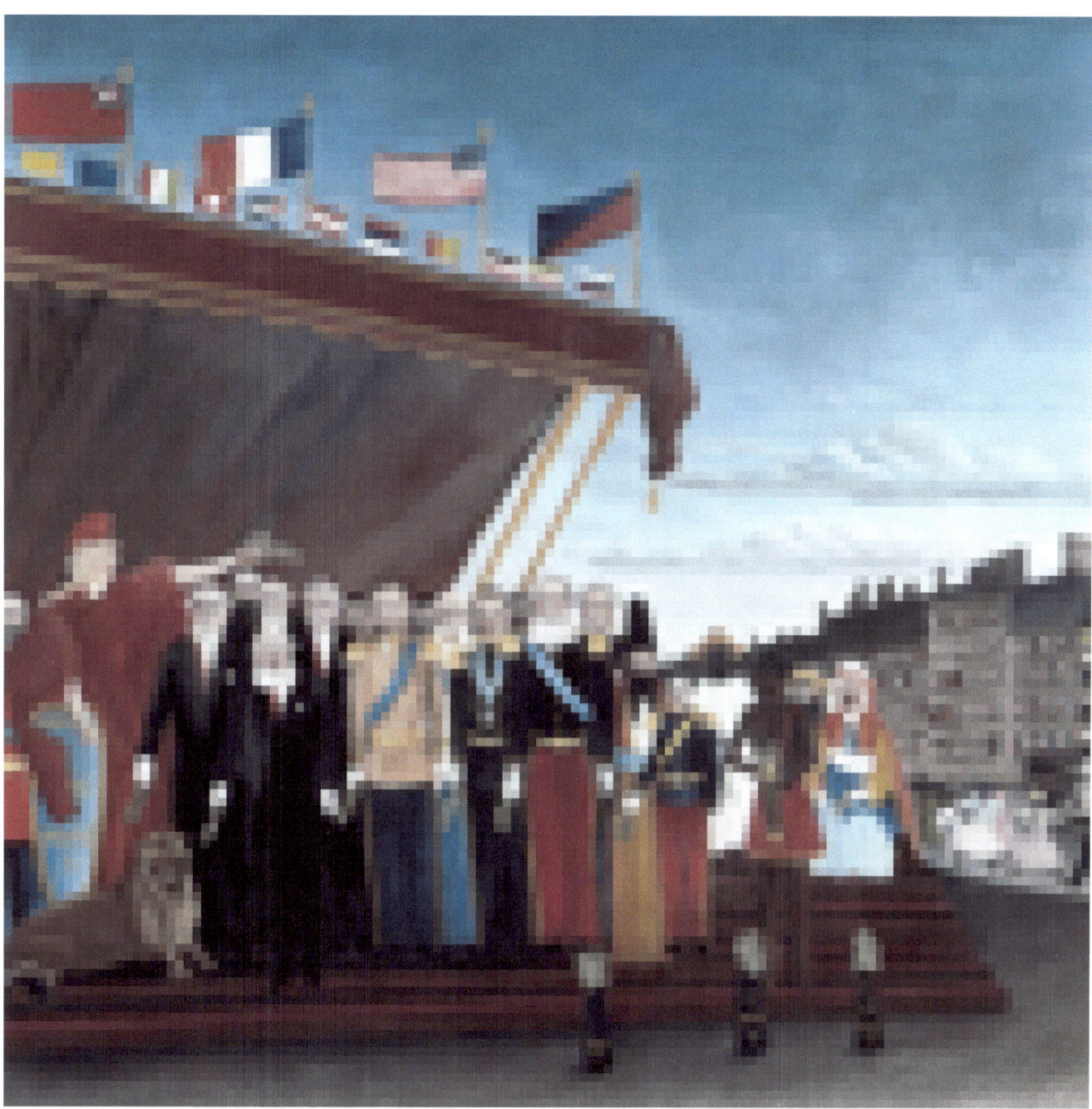

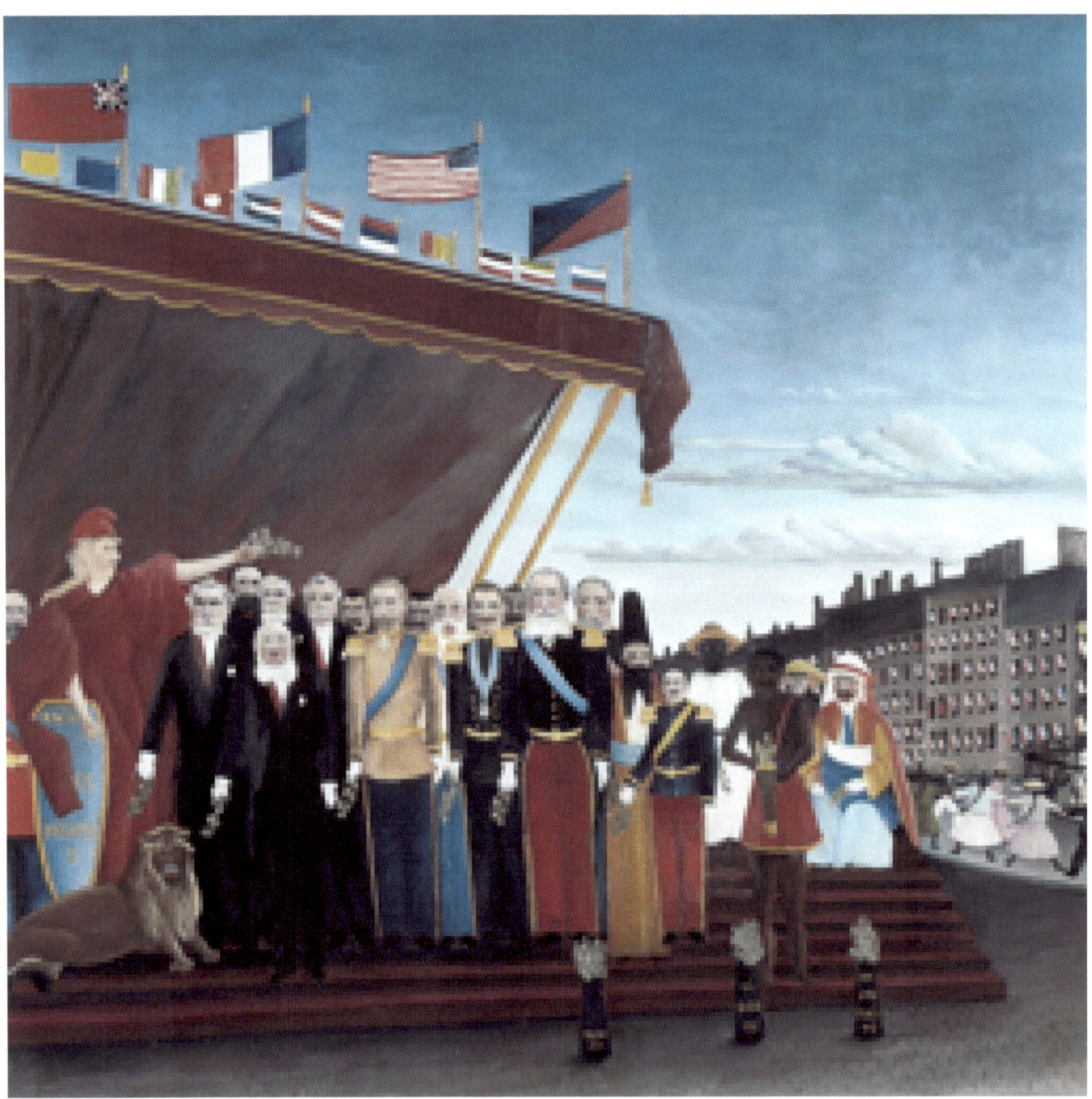

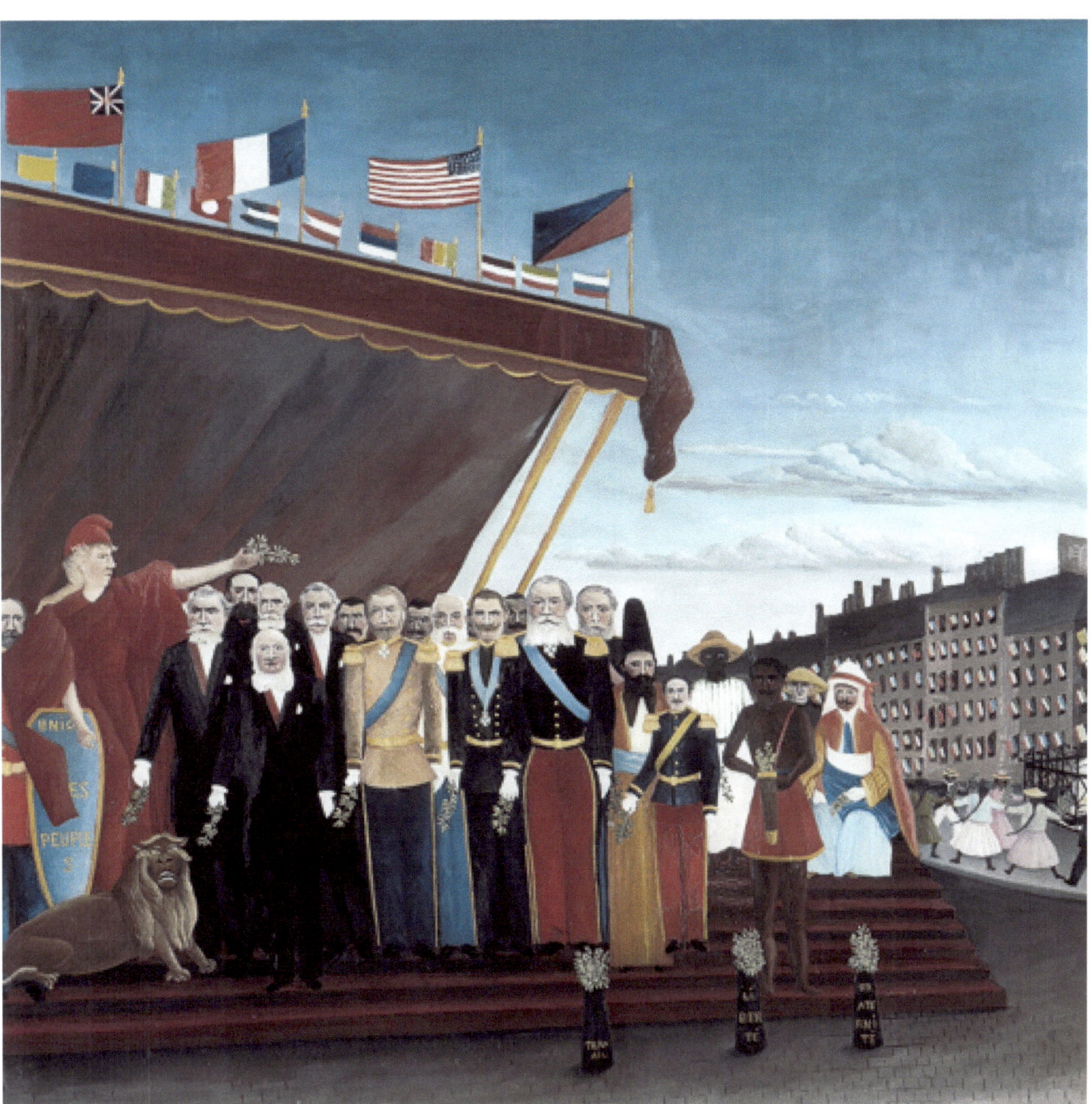

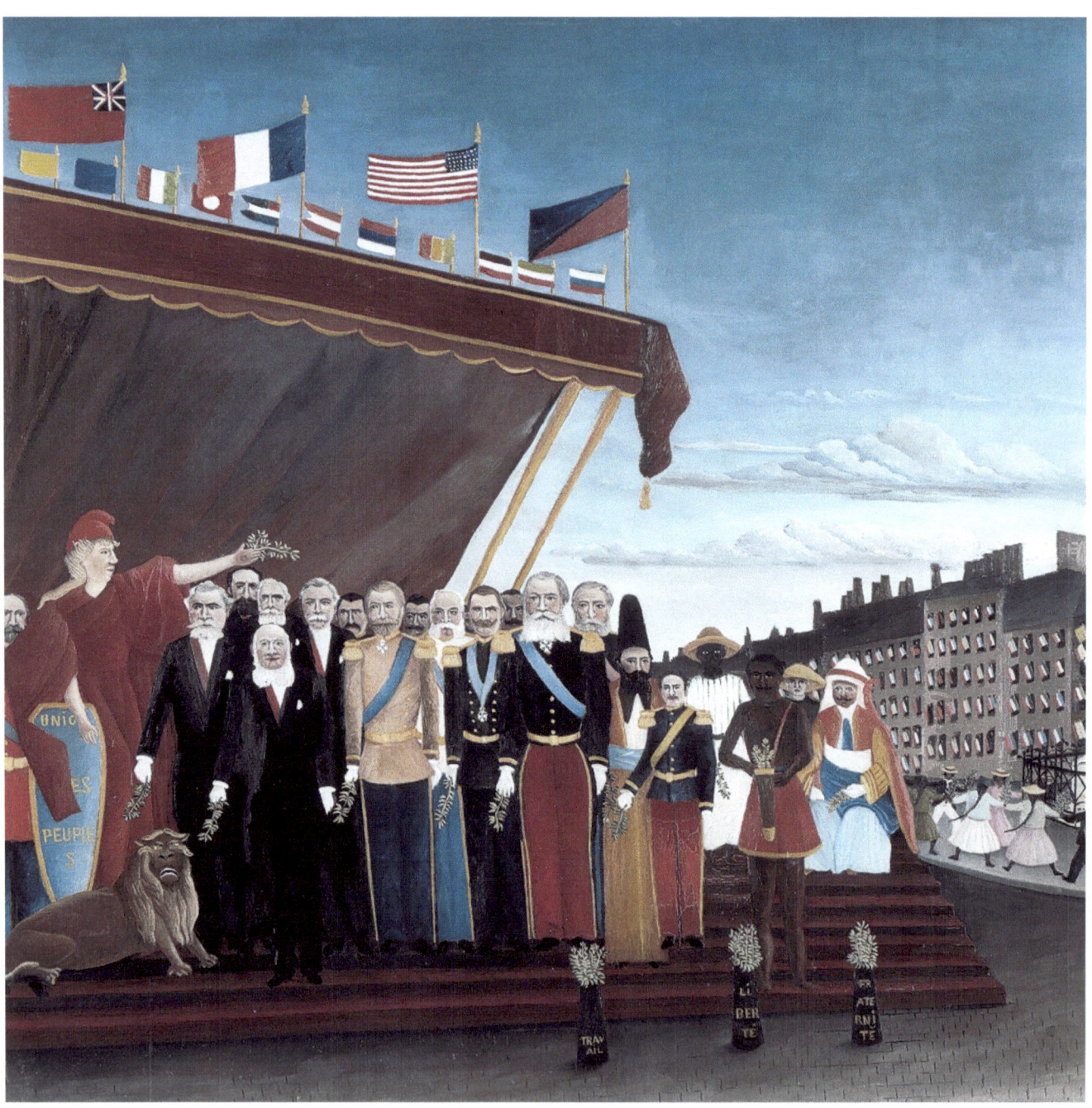

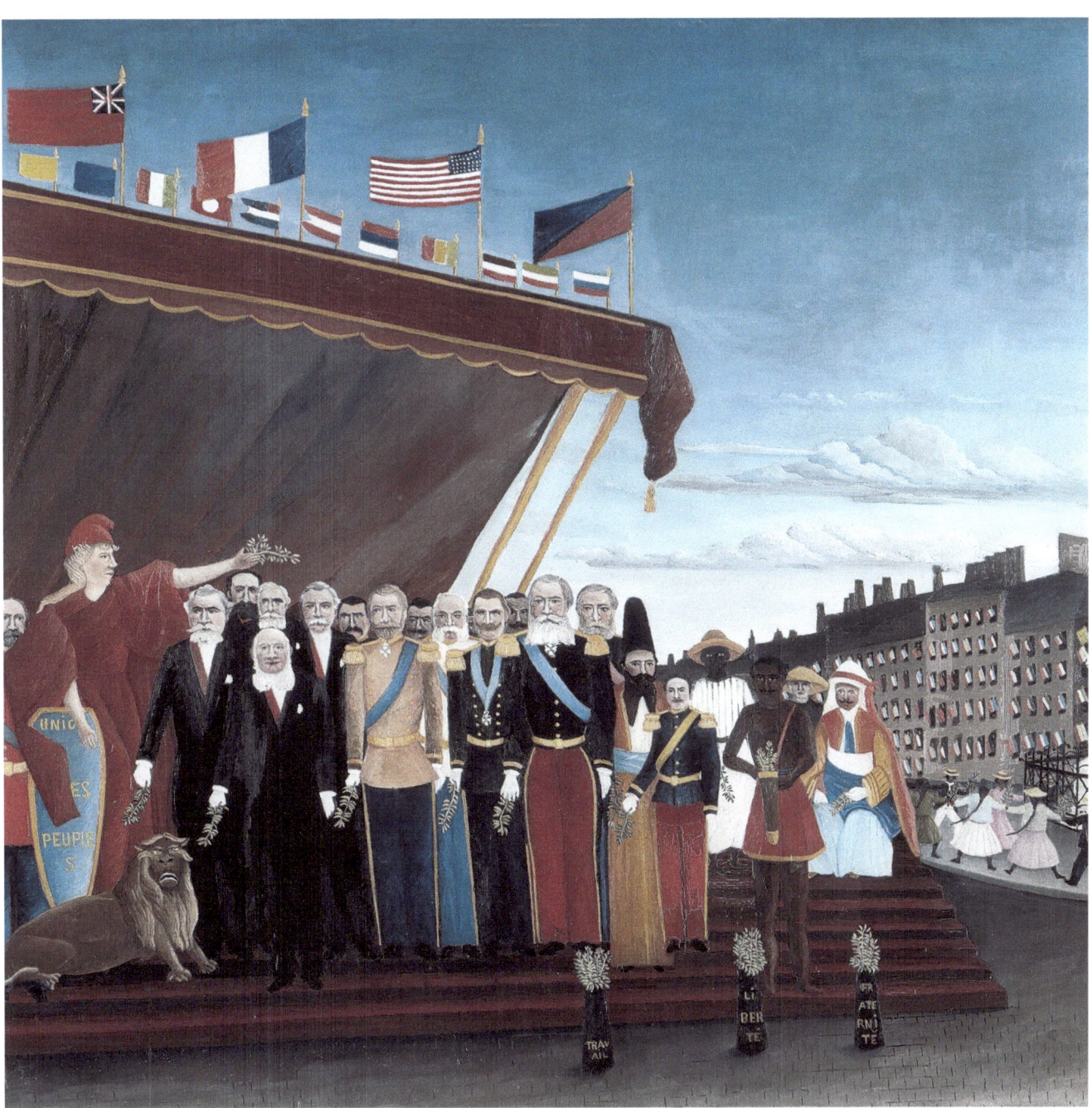

The Sleeping Gypsy

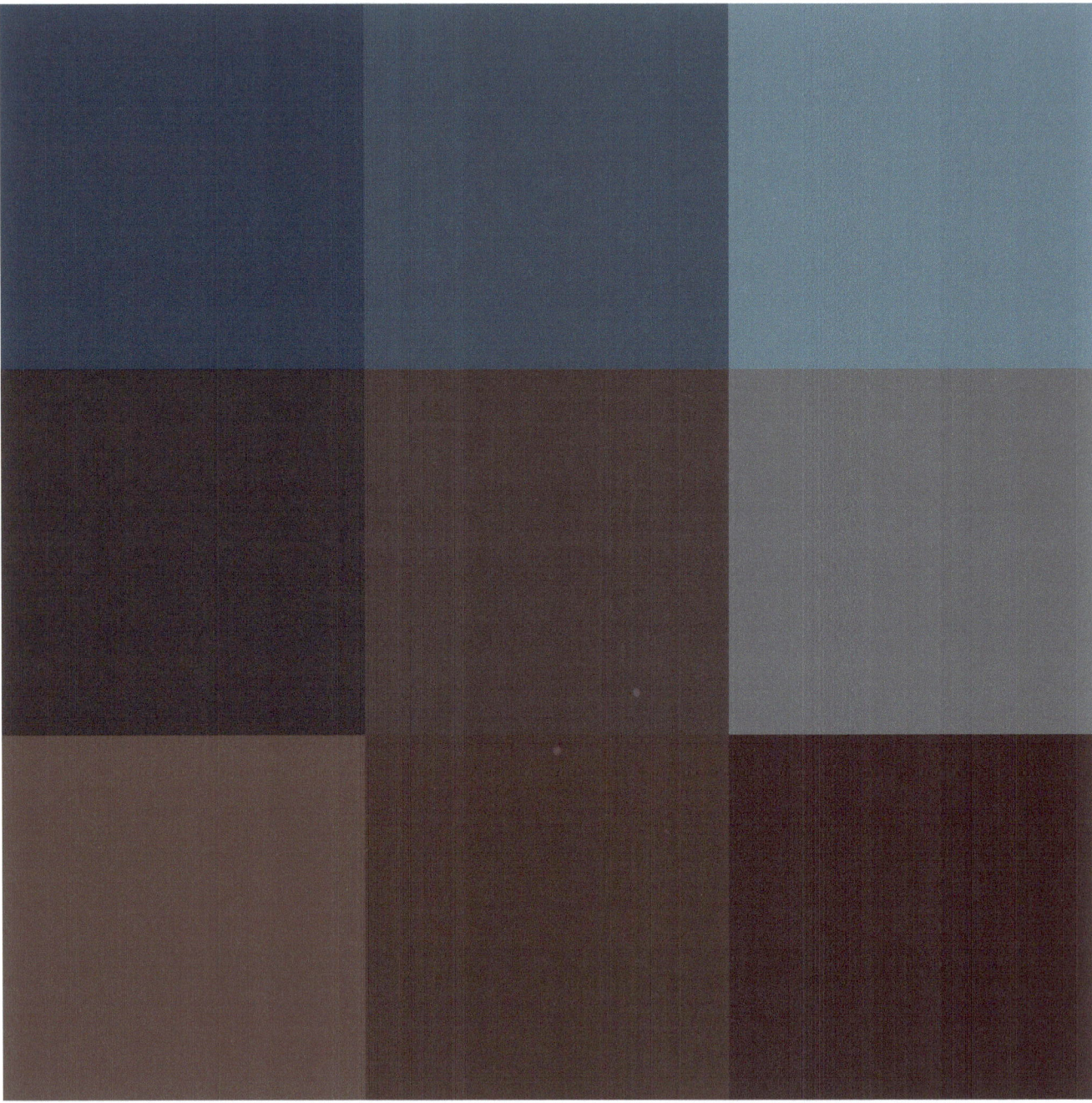

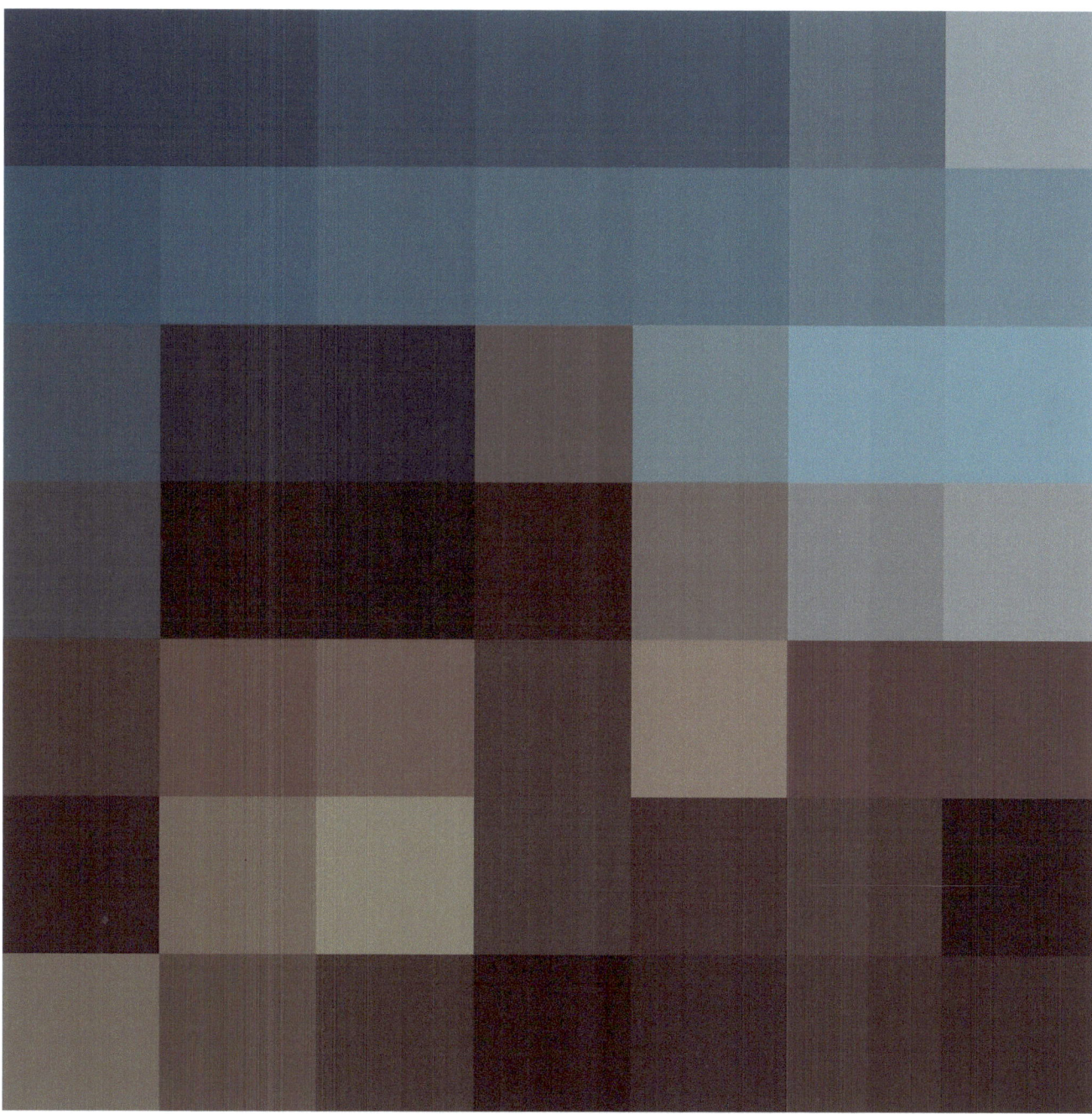

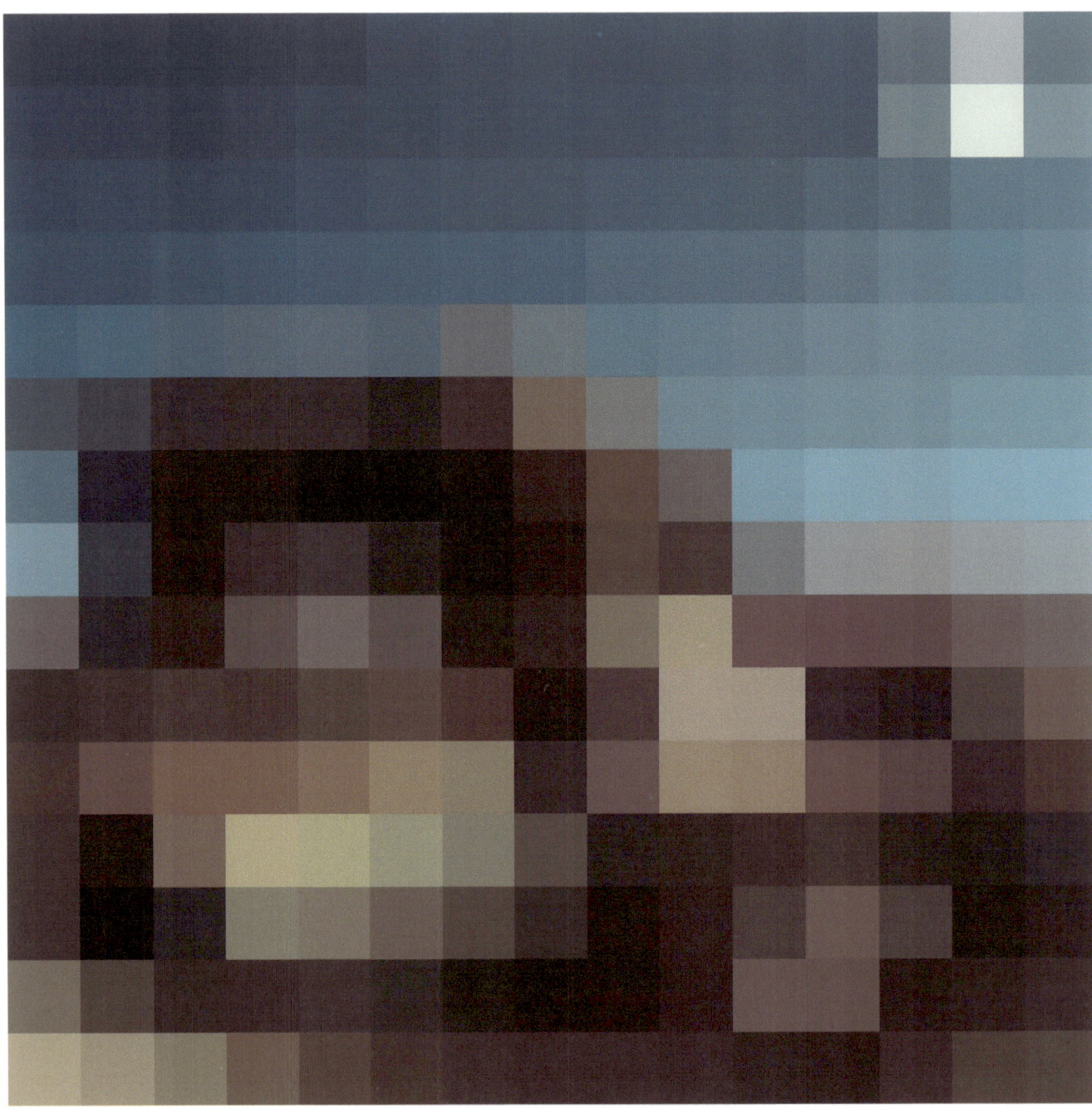

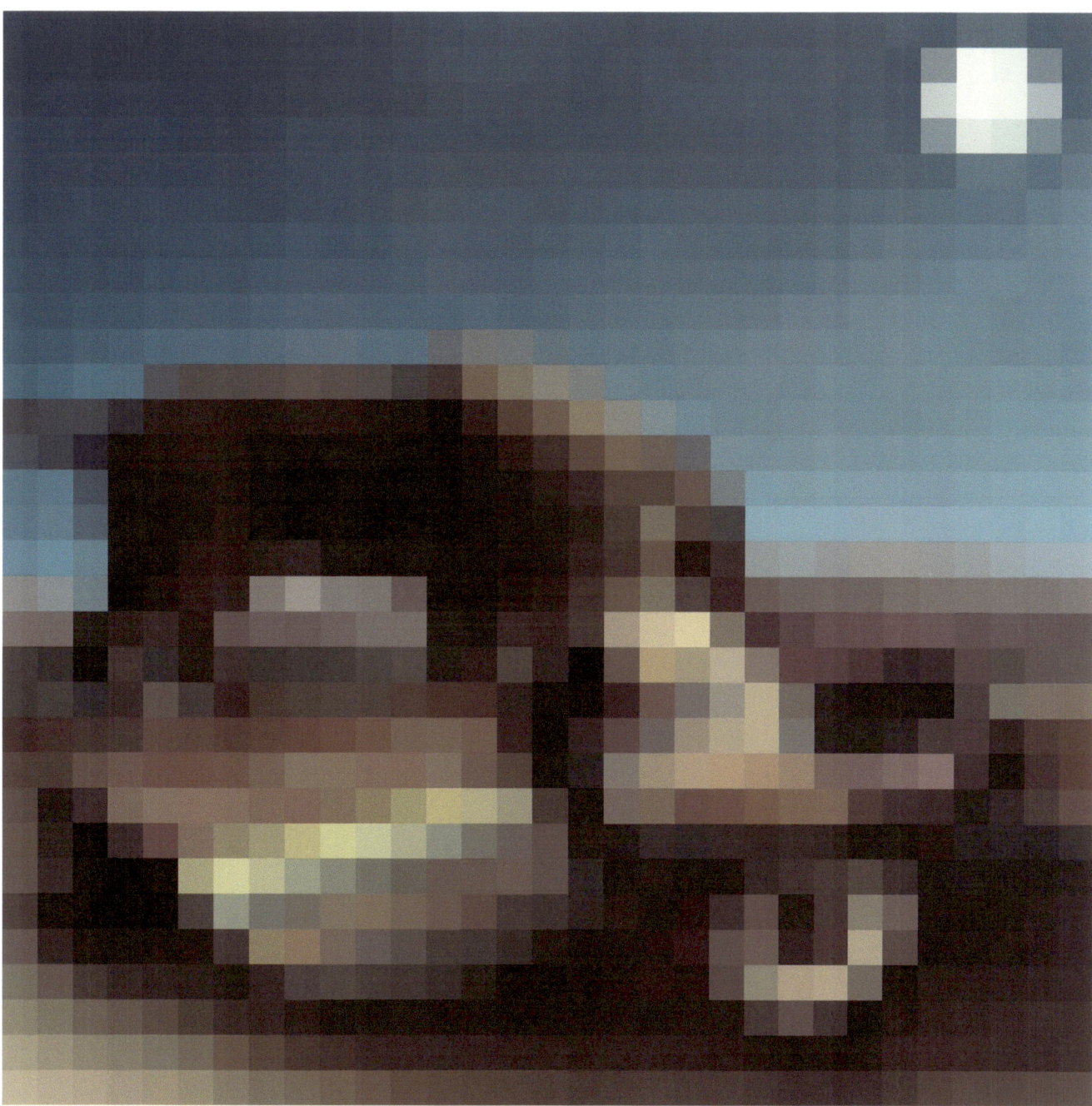

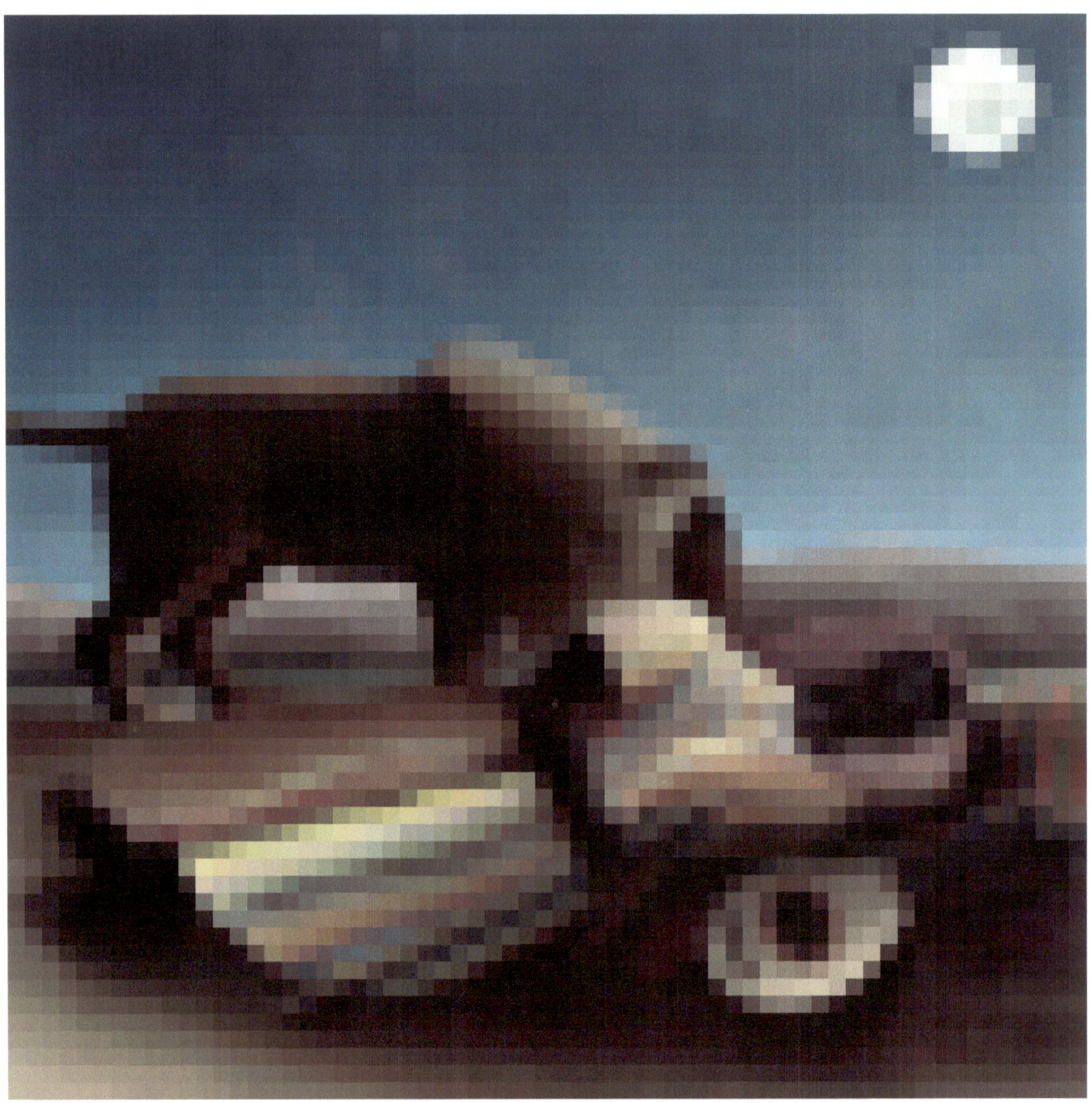

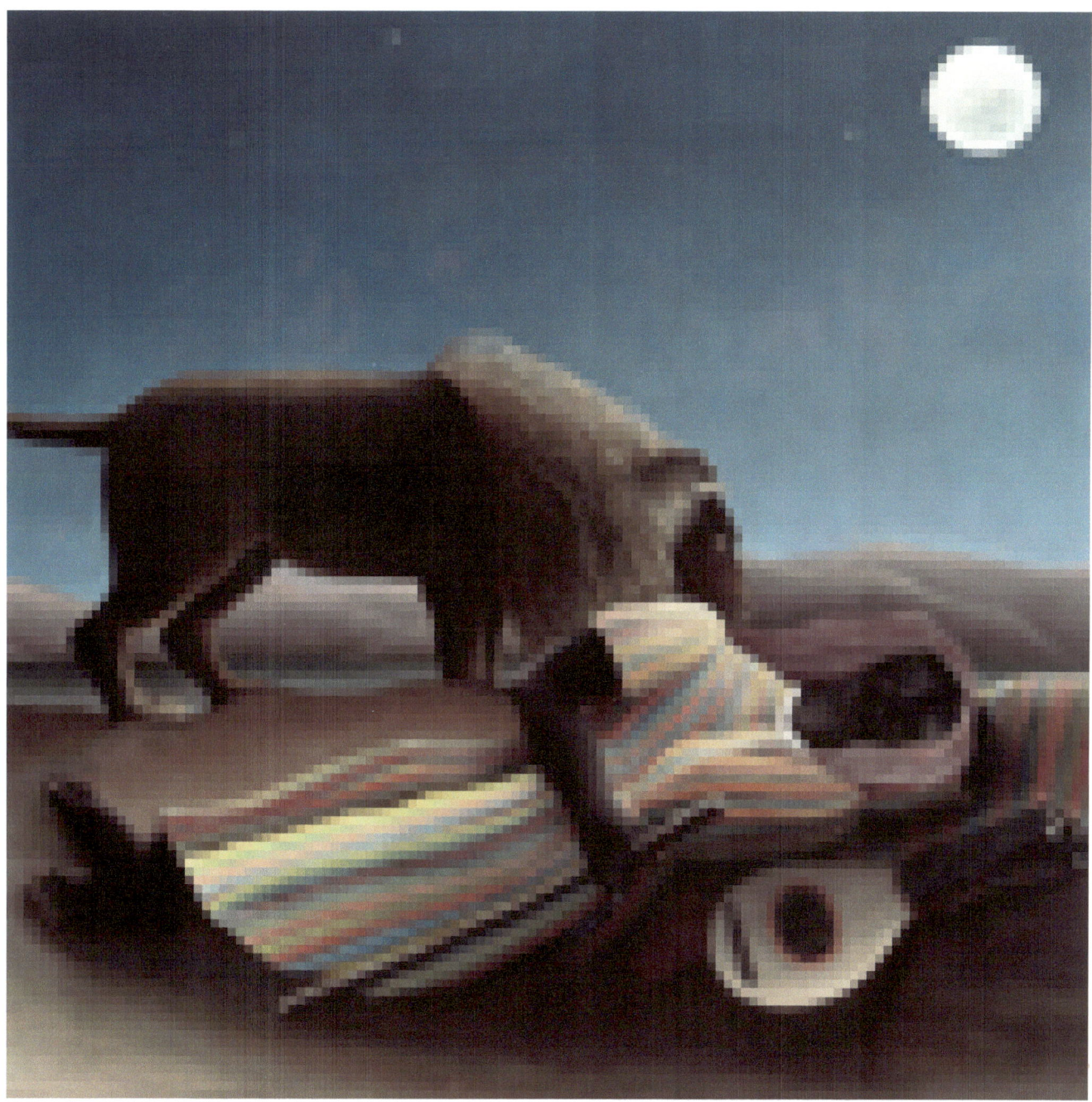

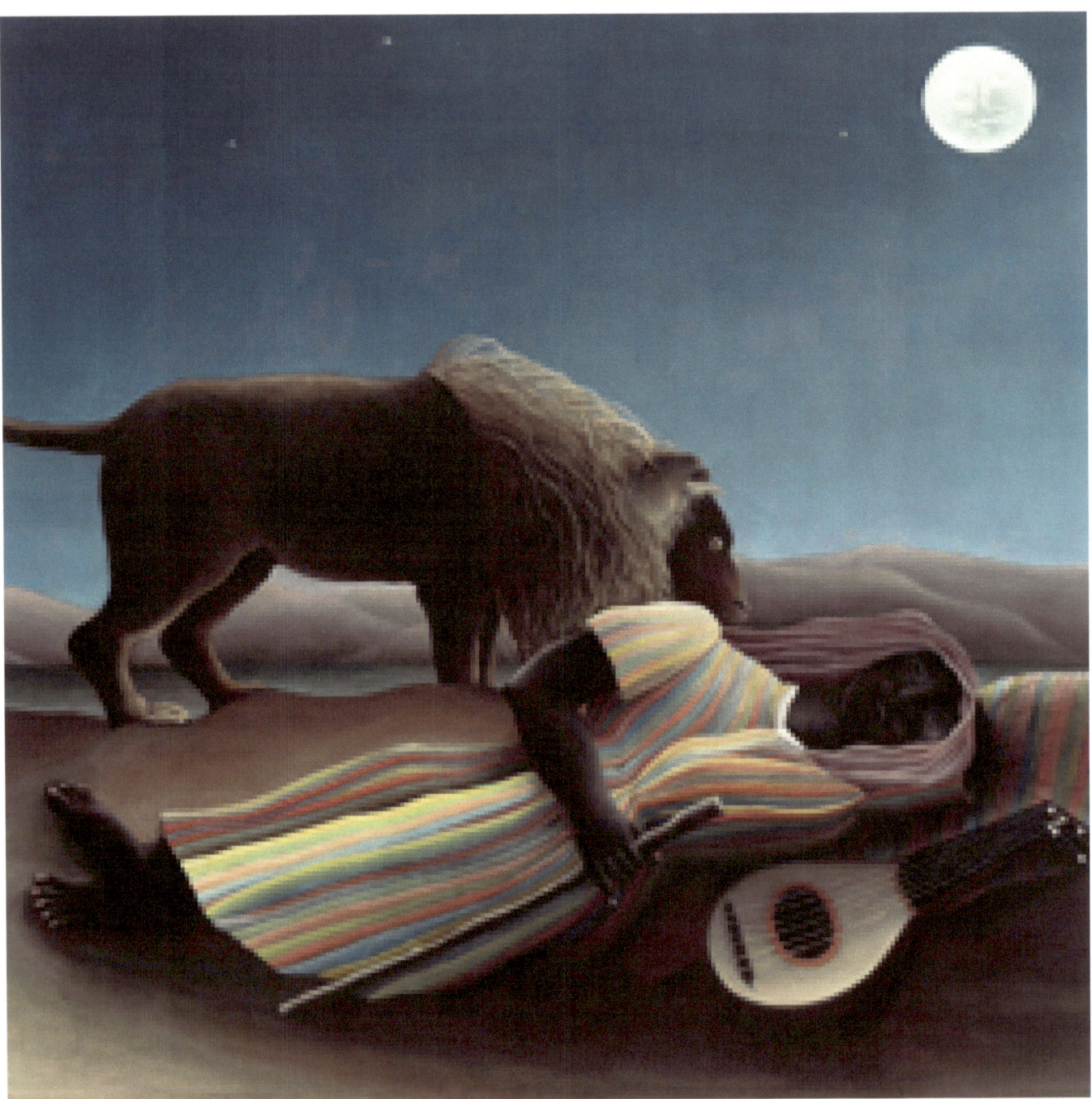

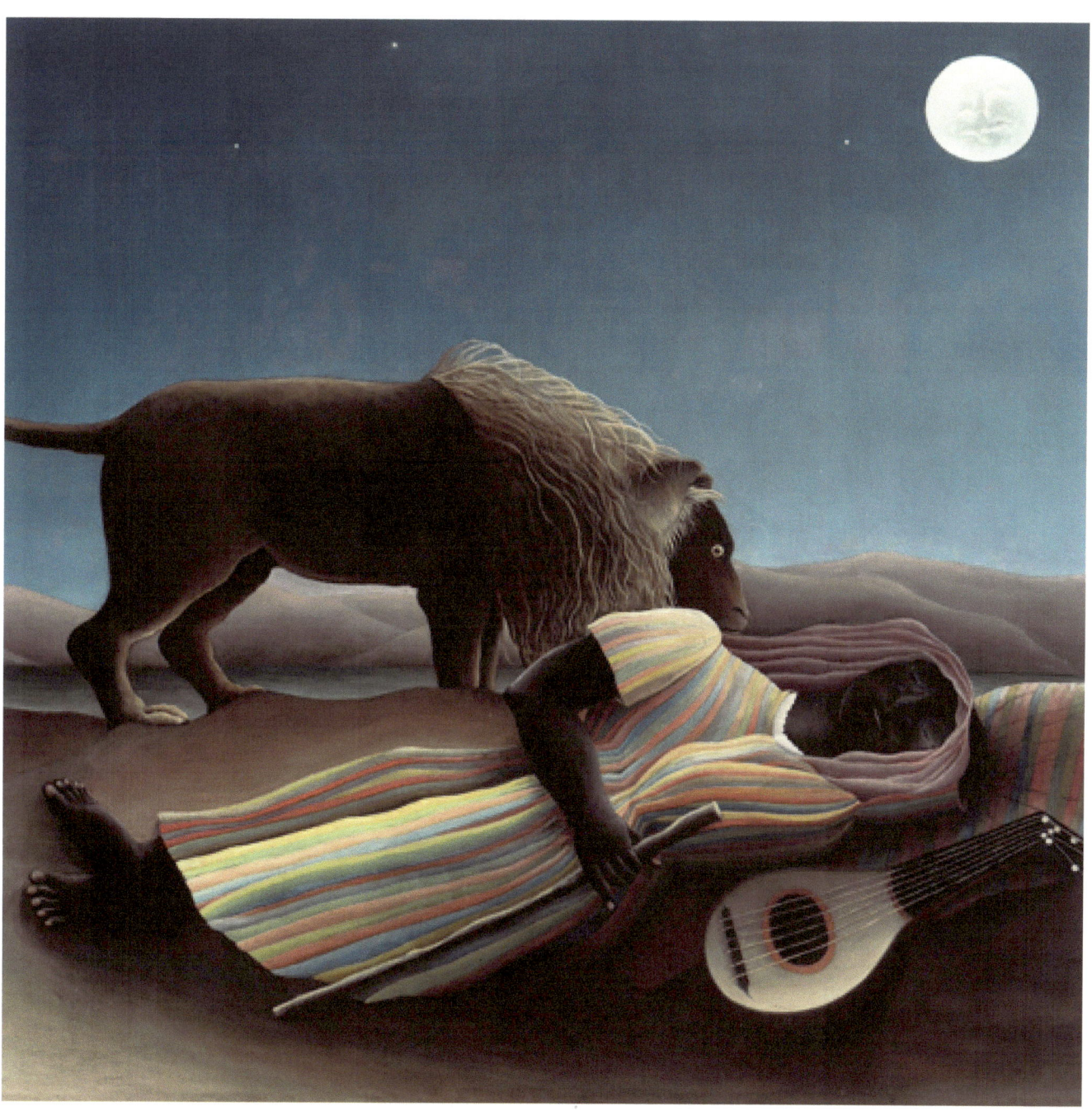

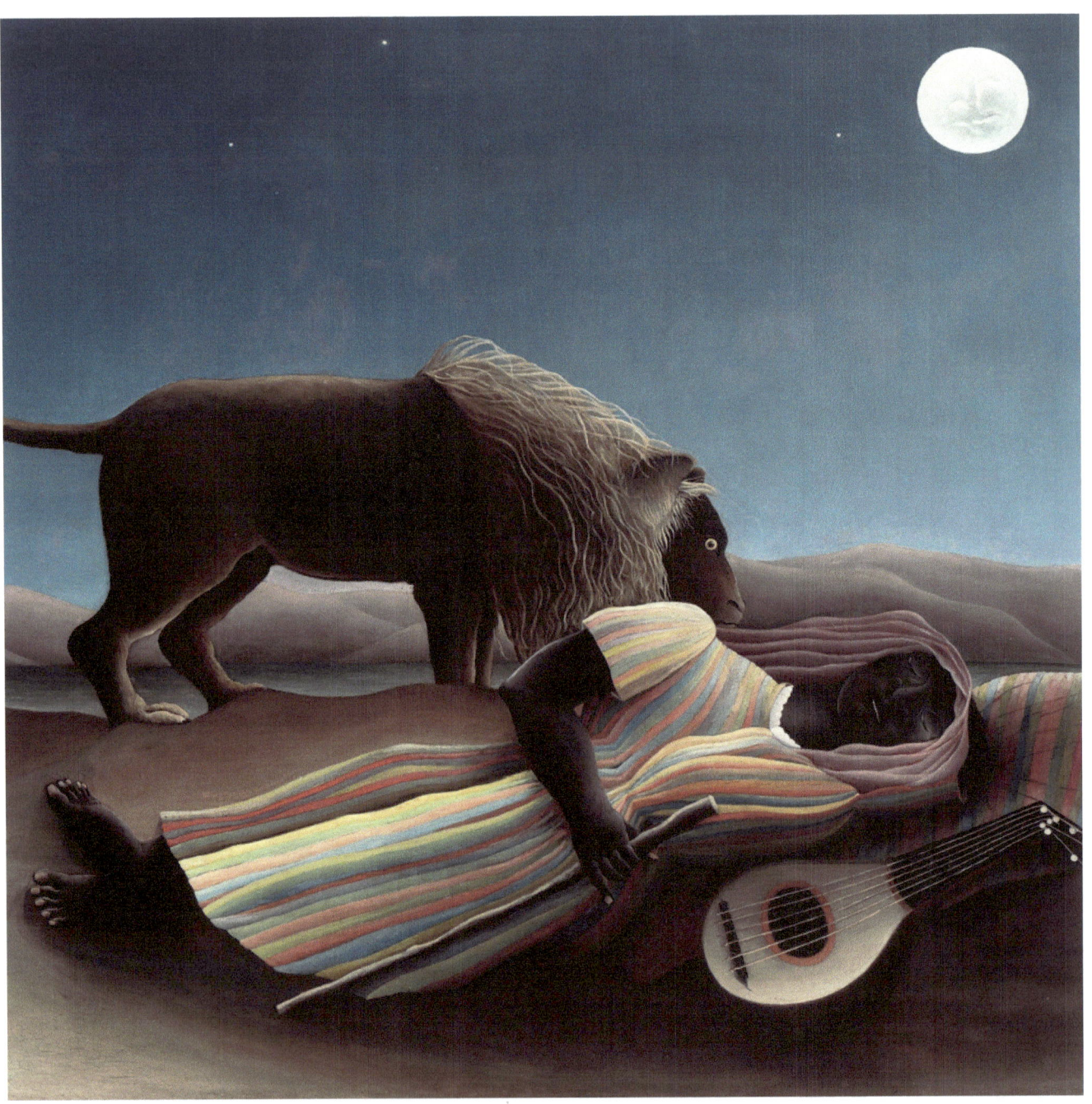

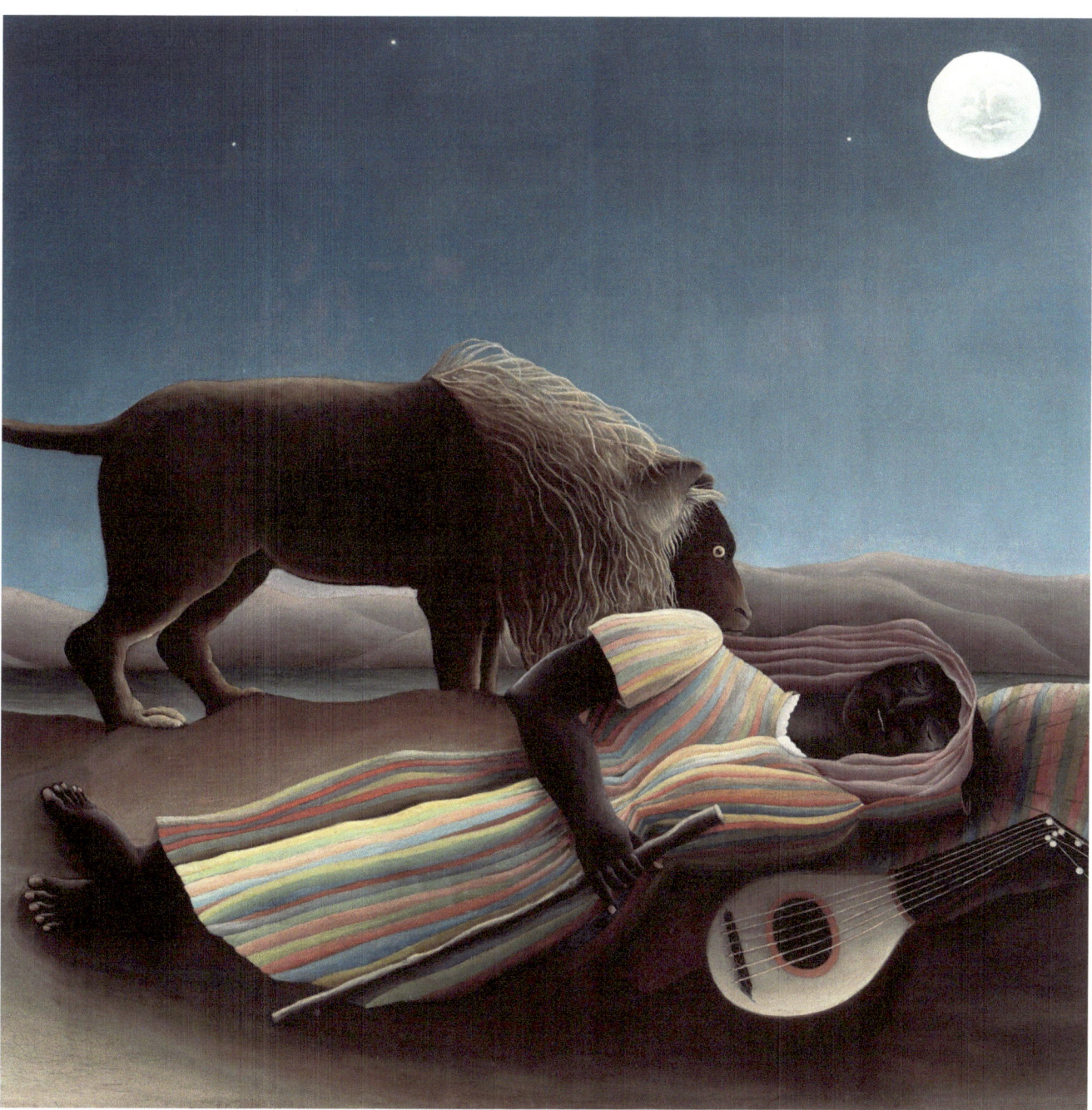

Tiger in a Tropical Storm

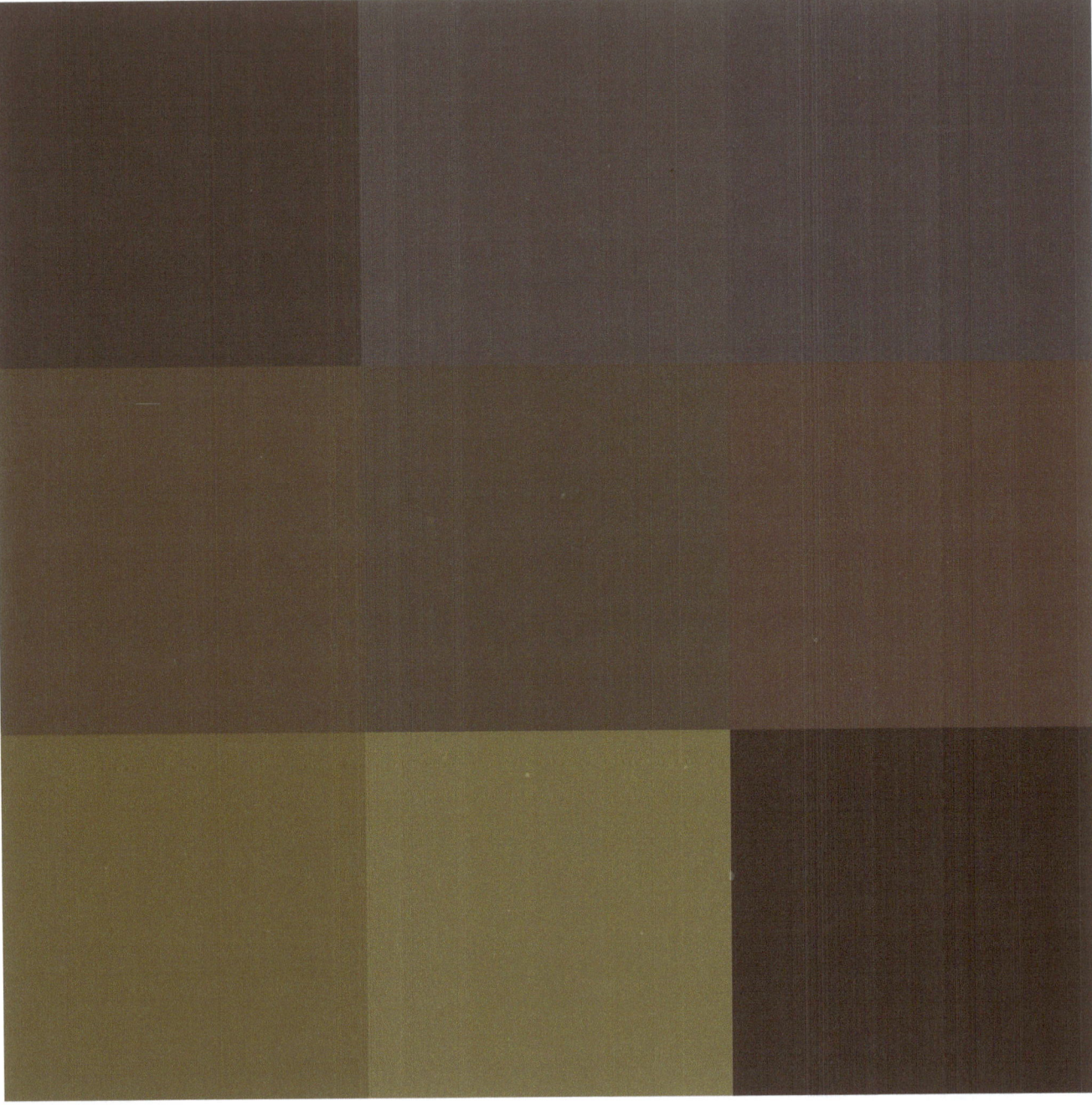

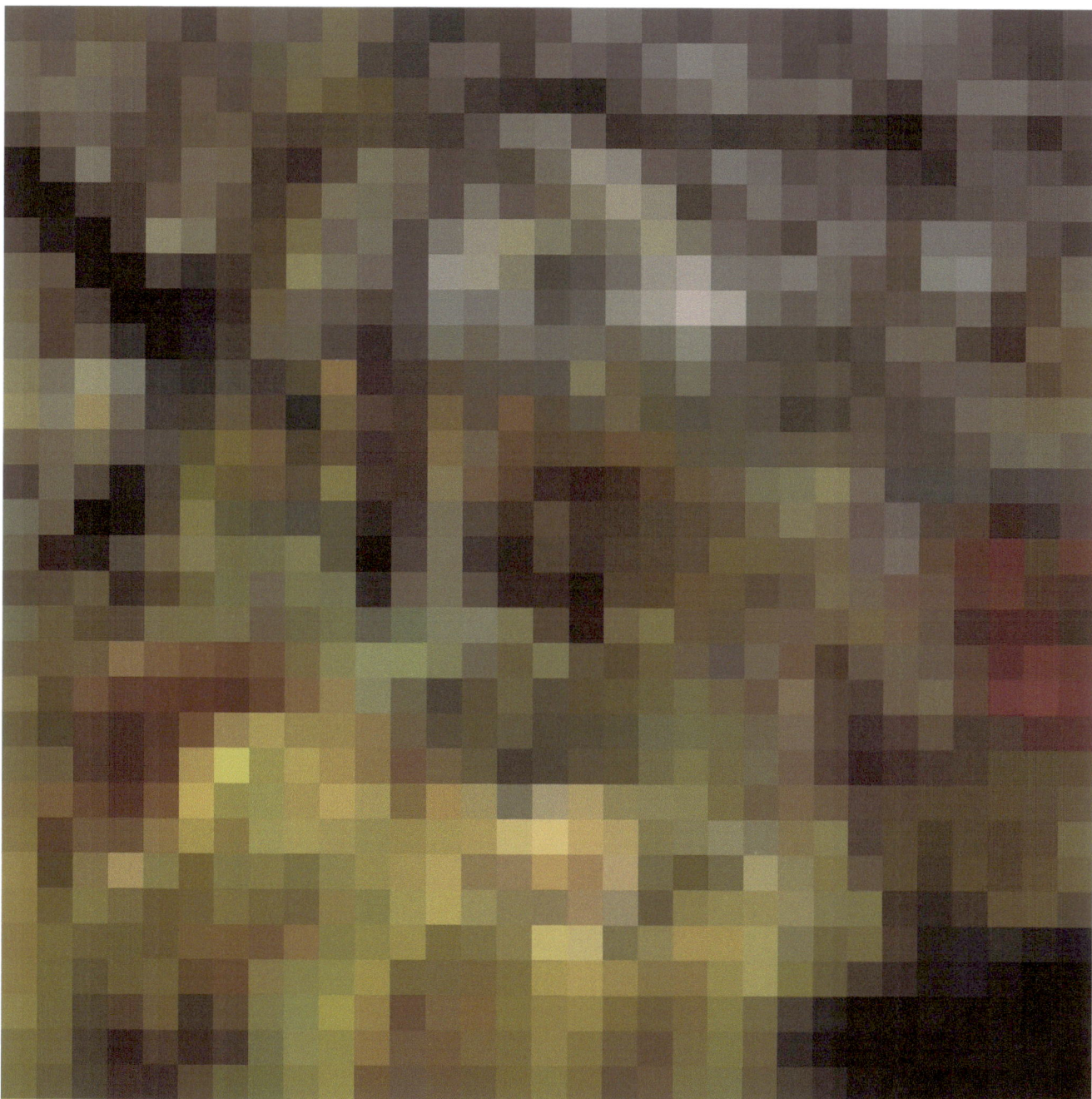

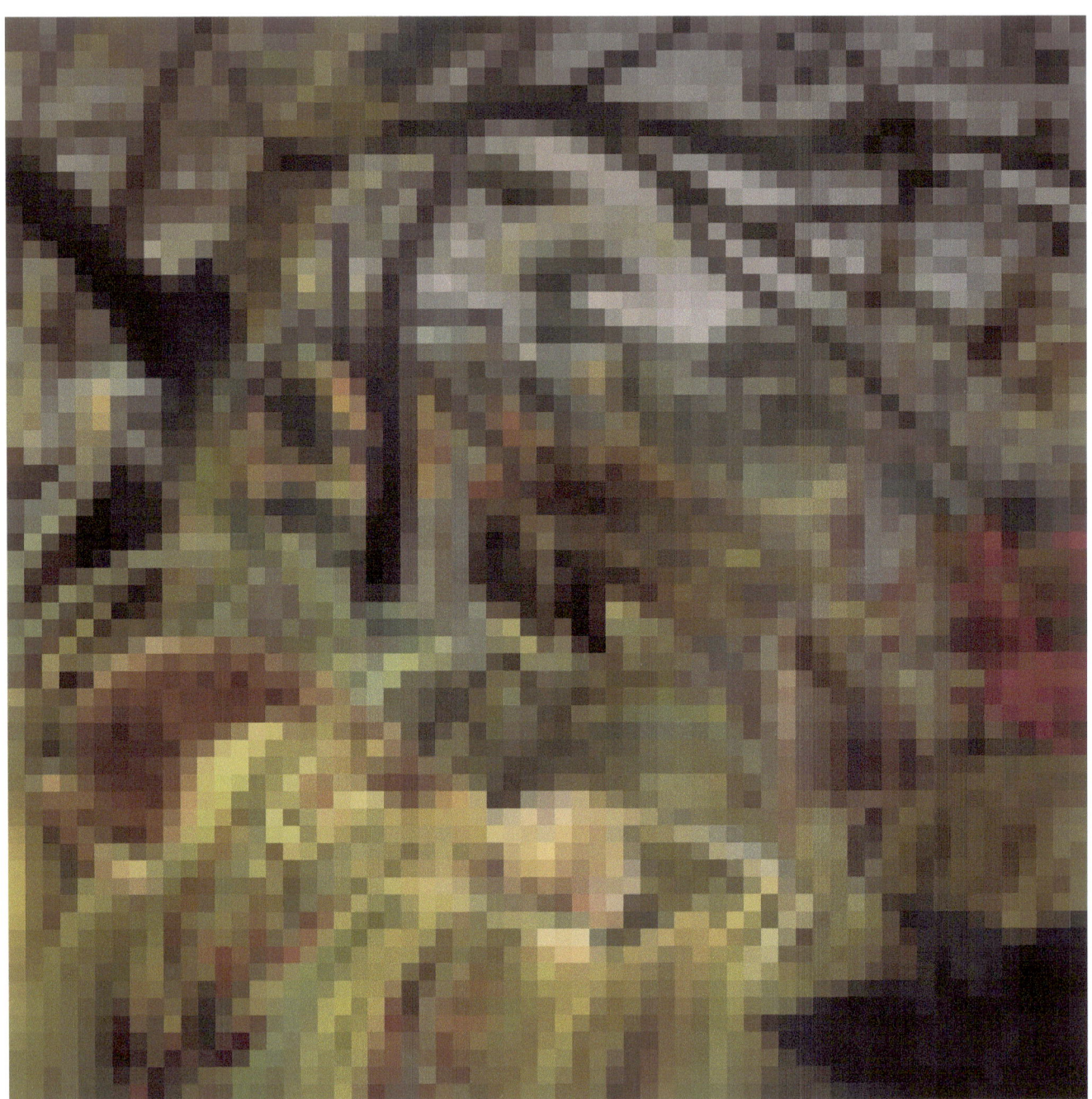

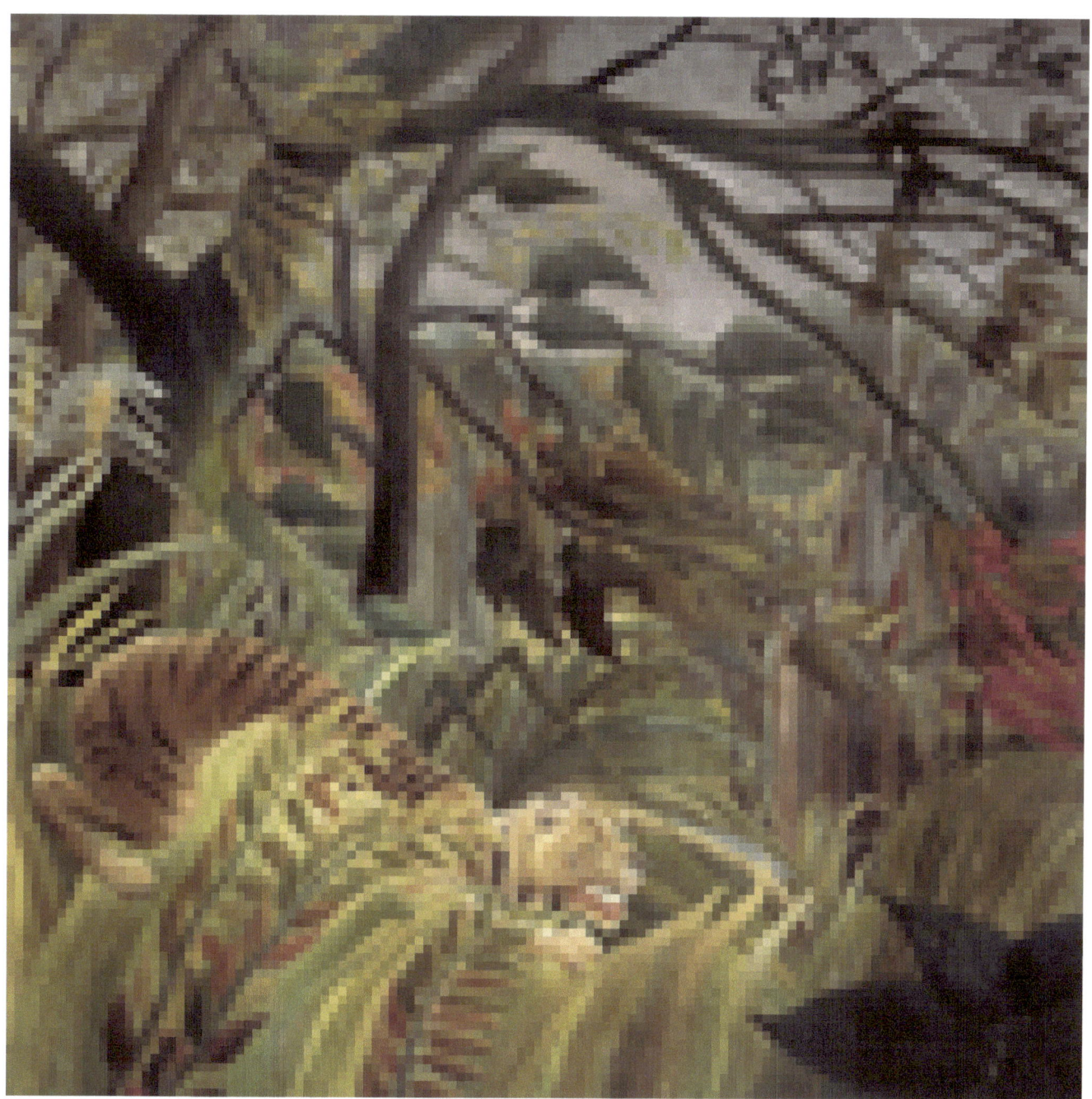

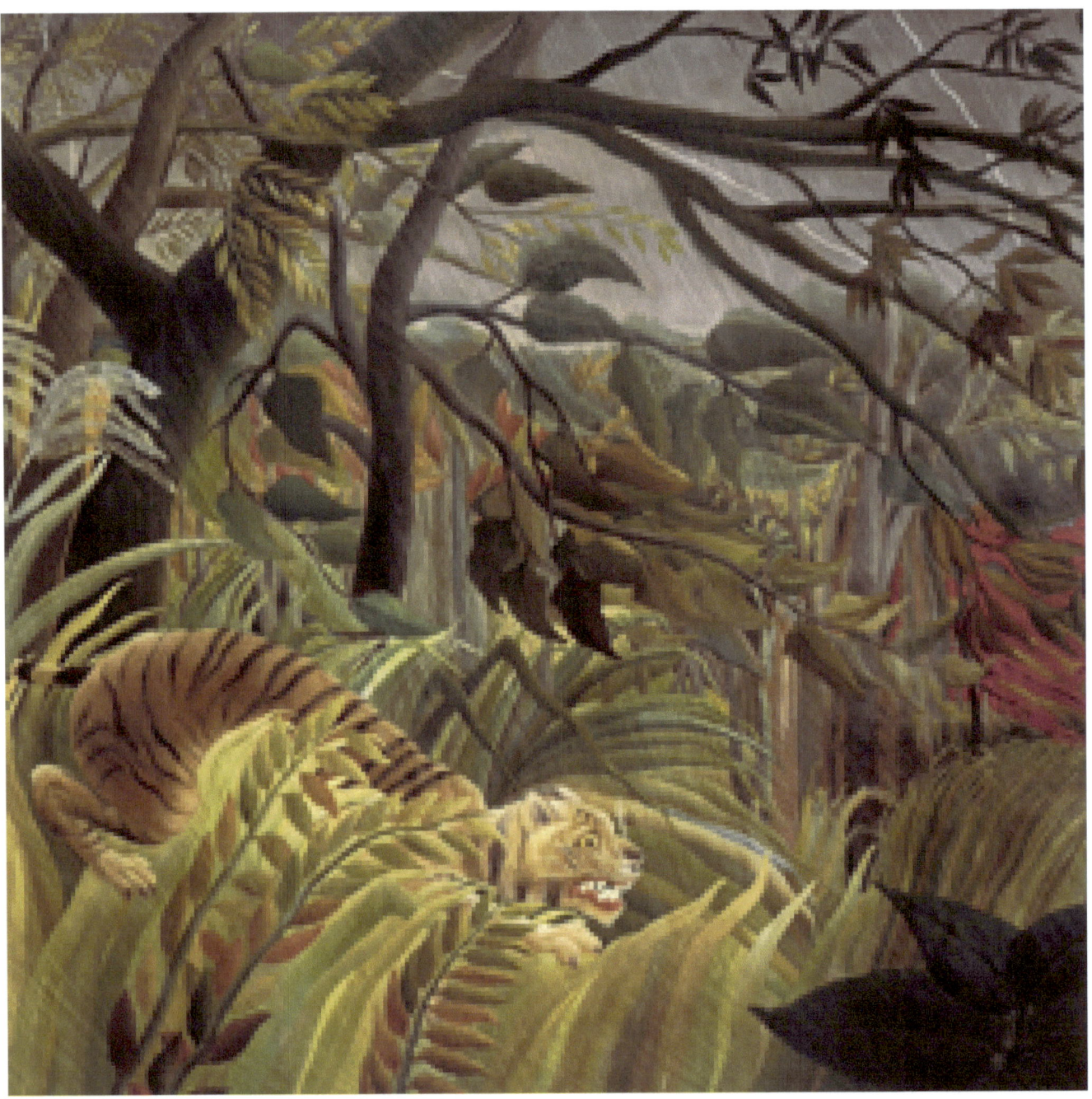

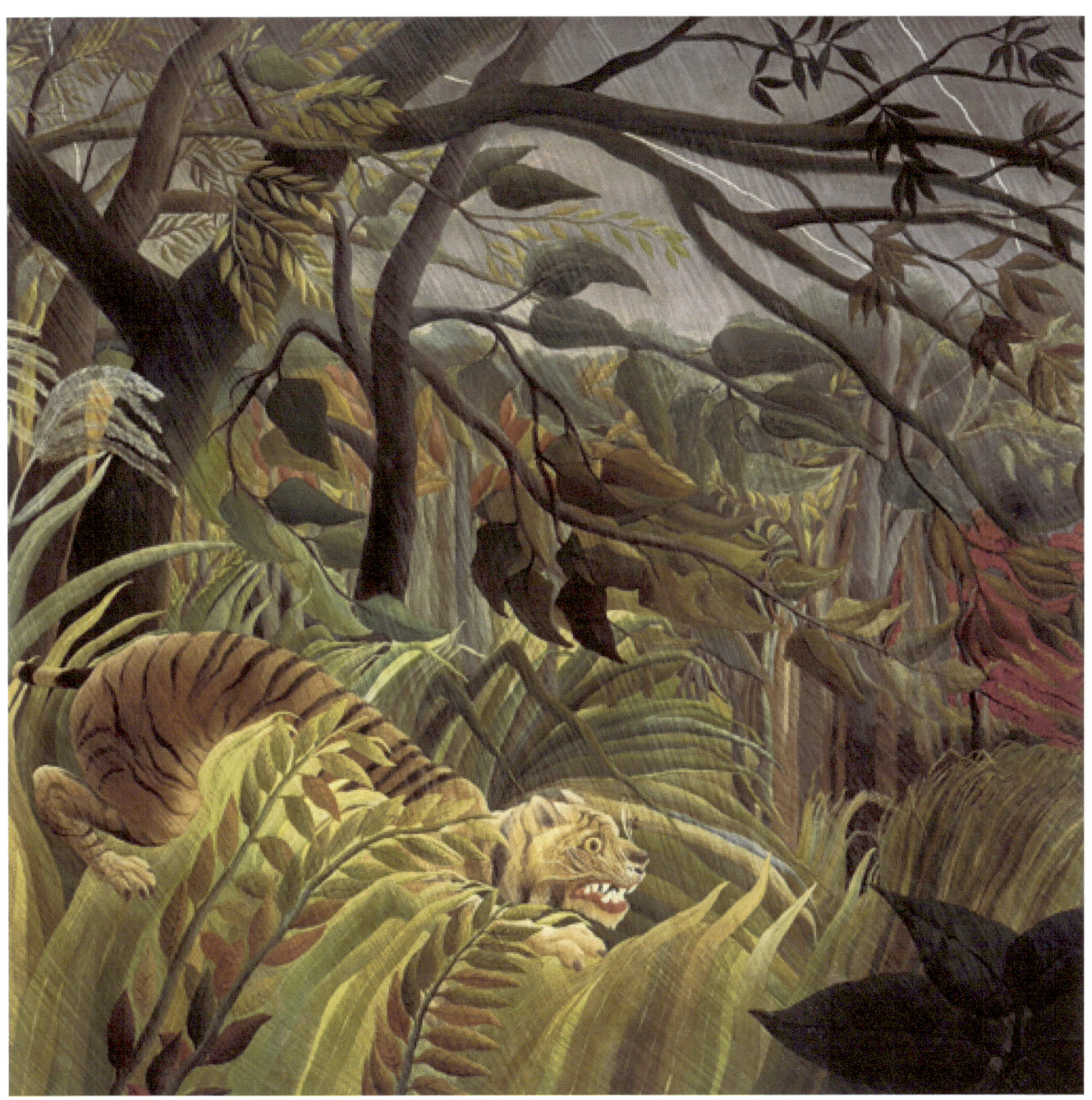

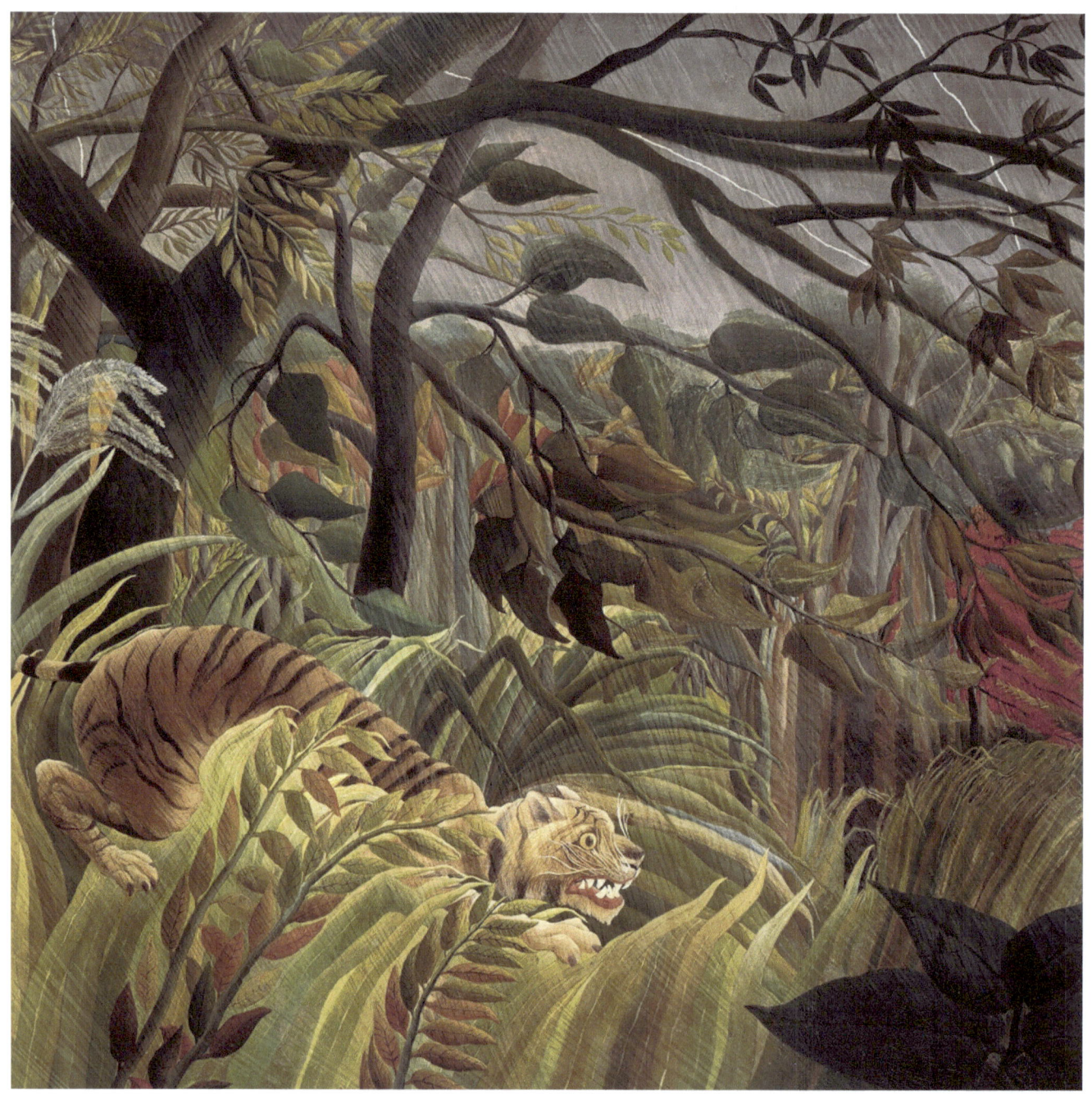

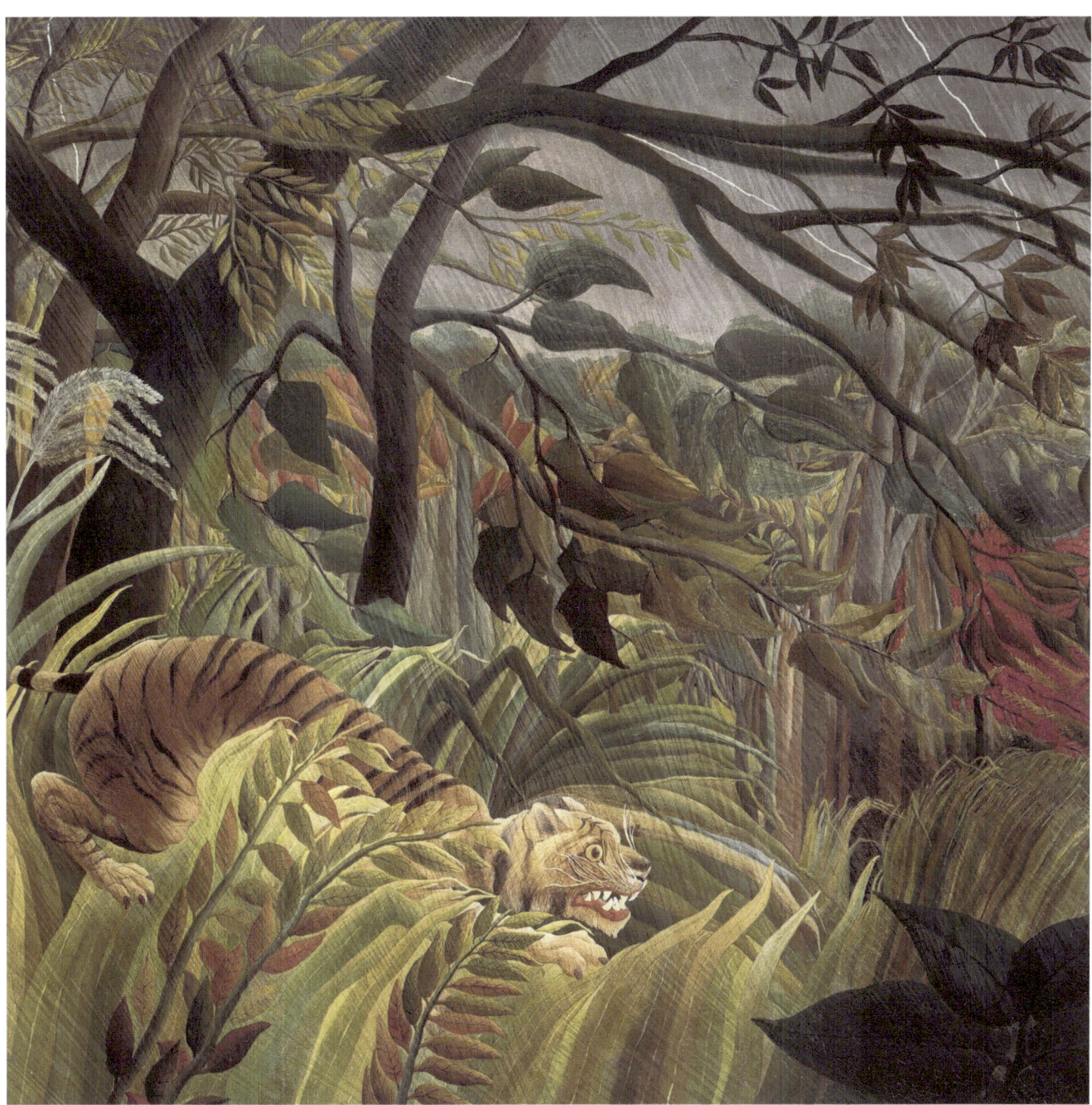

 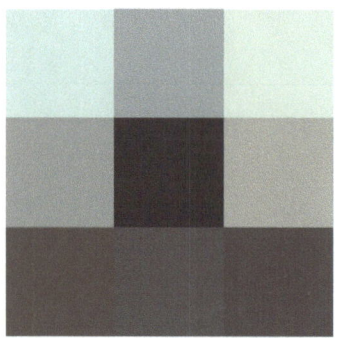 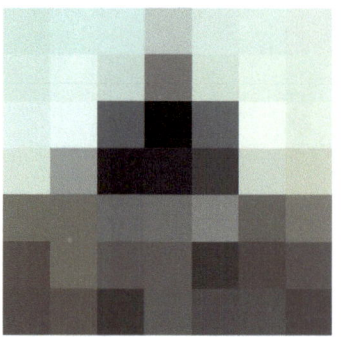

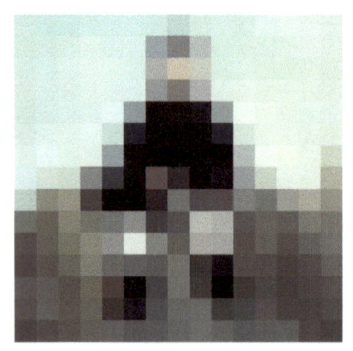 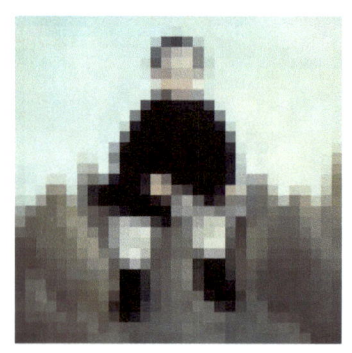 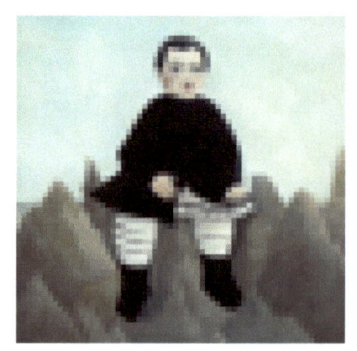

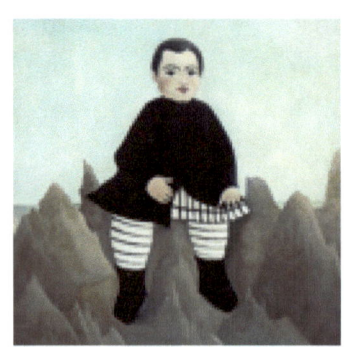 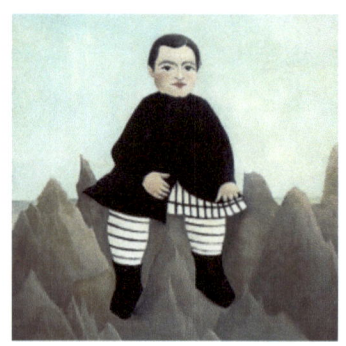 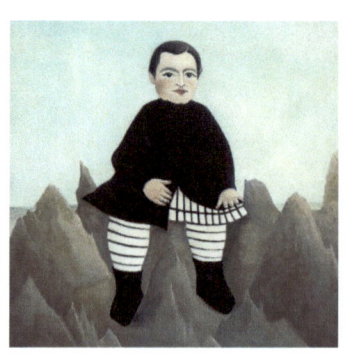

 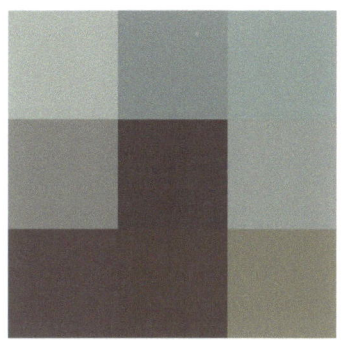 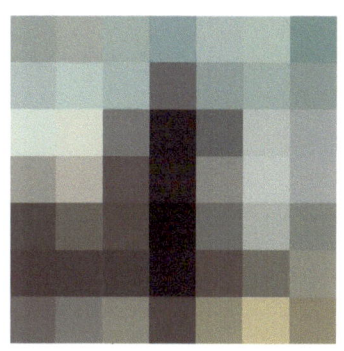

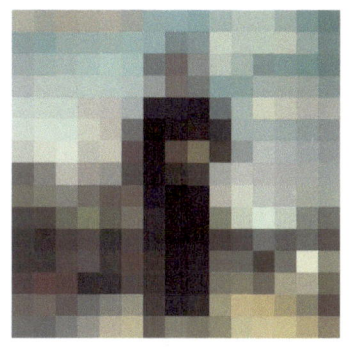 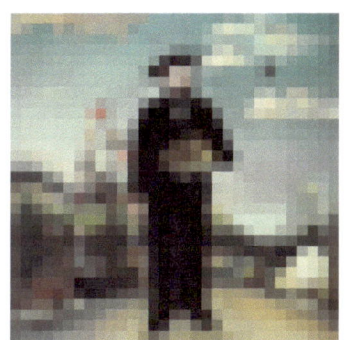 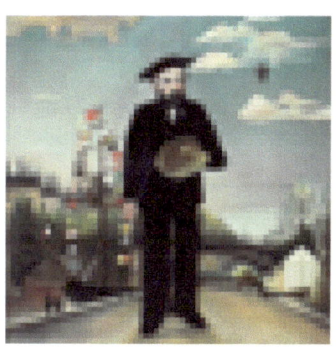

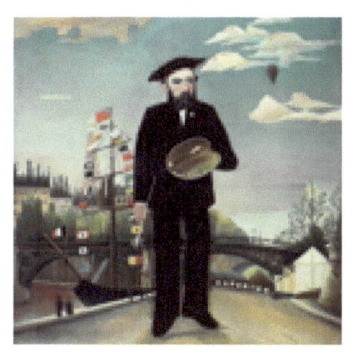 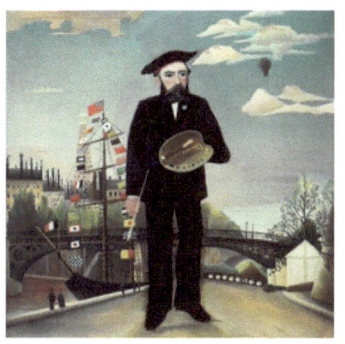 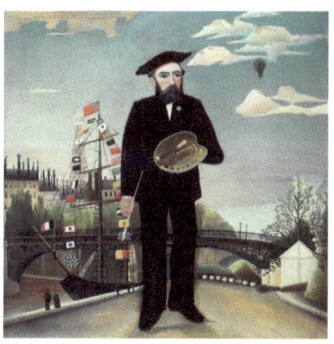

 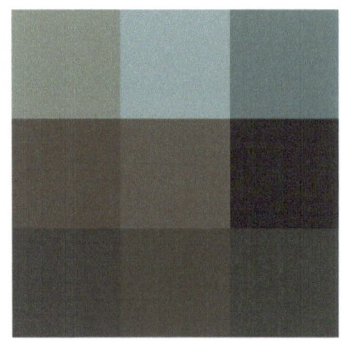 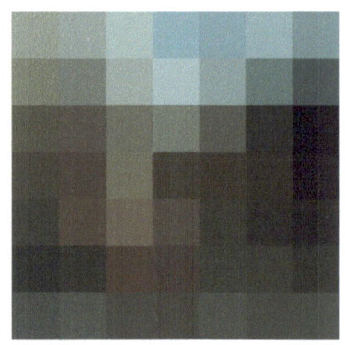

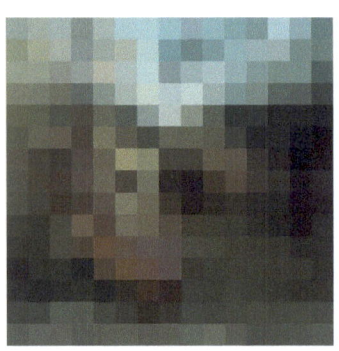 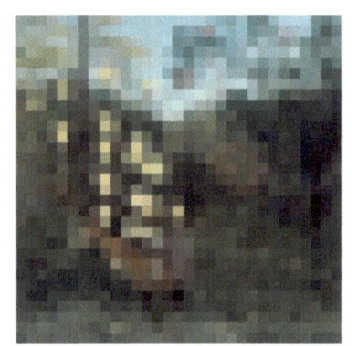 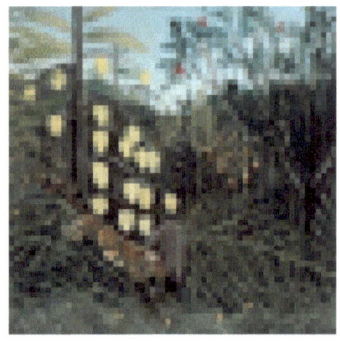

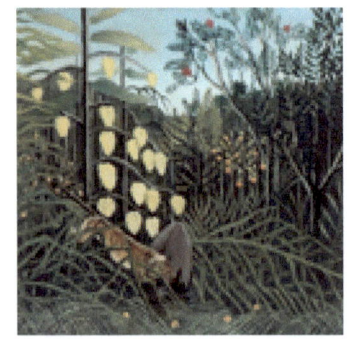 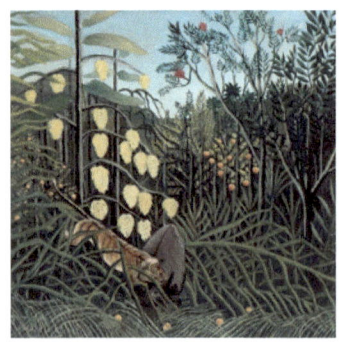 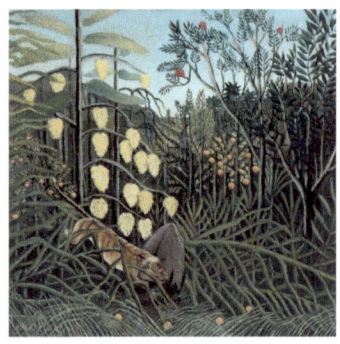

 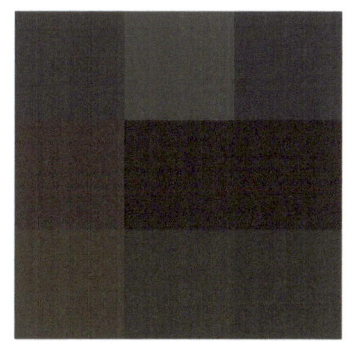 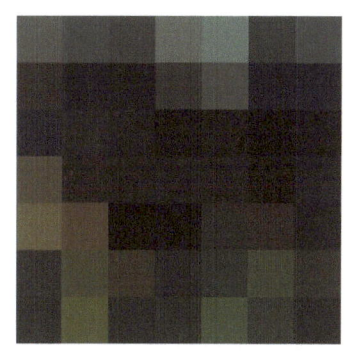

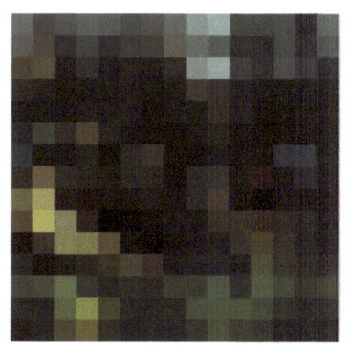 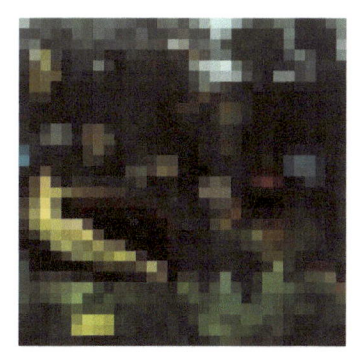 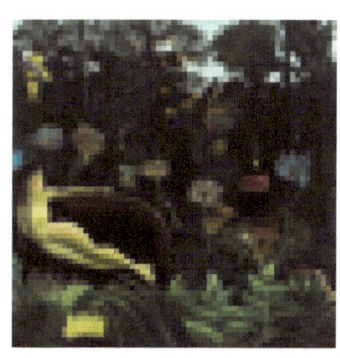

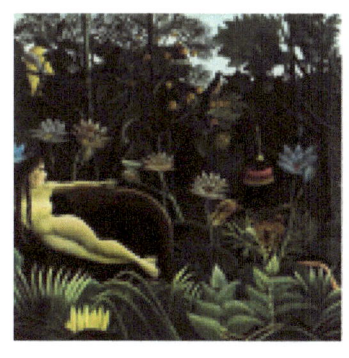 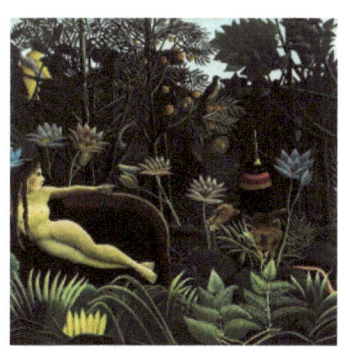 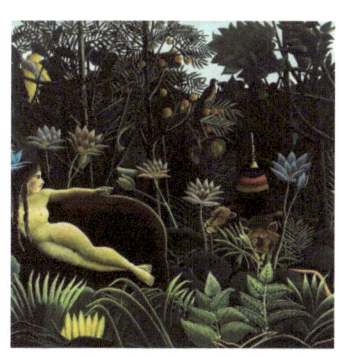

 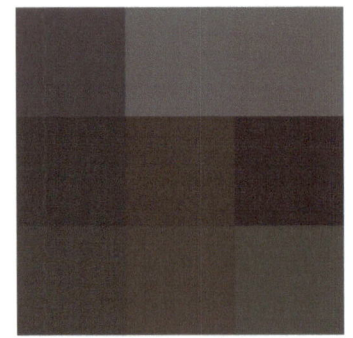 

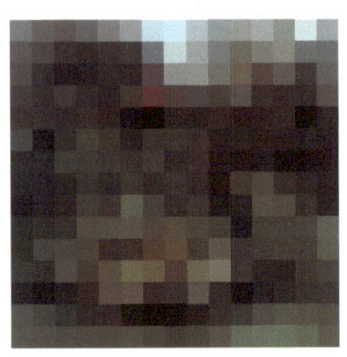 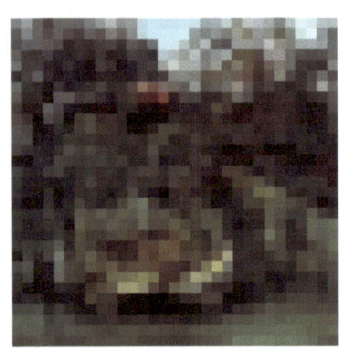 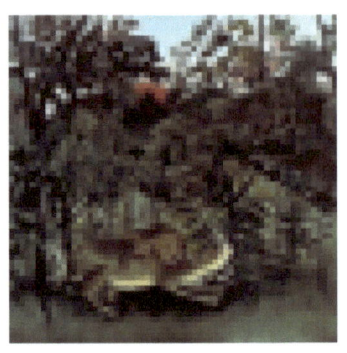

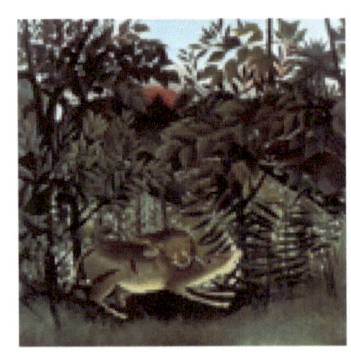 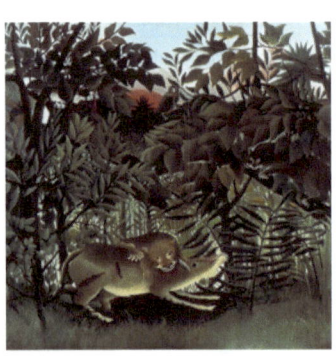 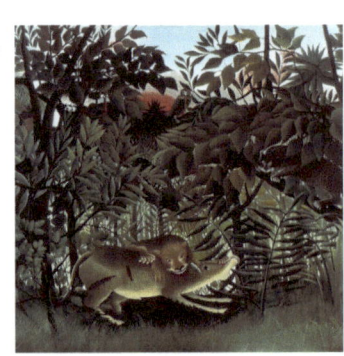

 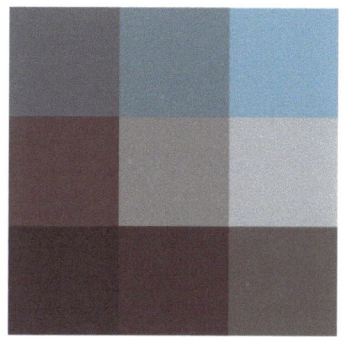 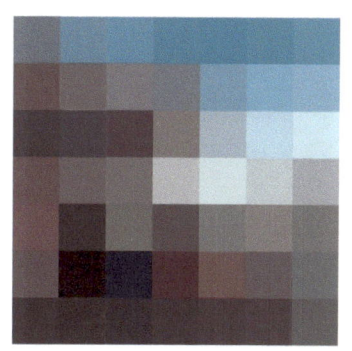
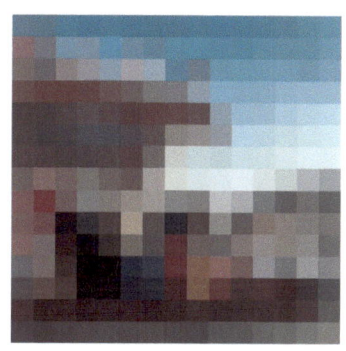 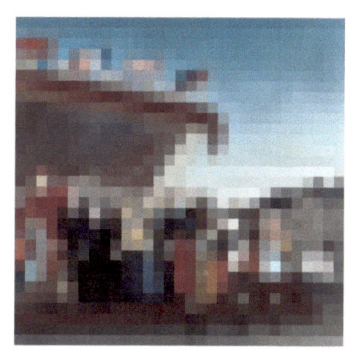 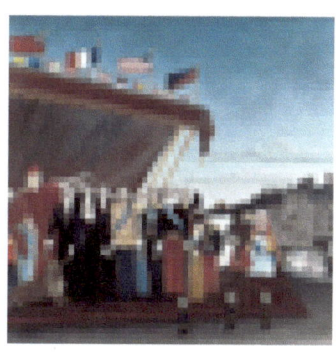
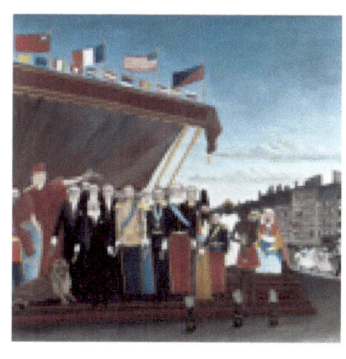 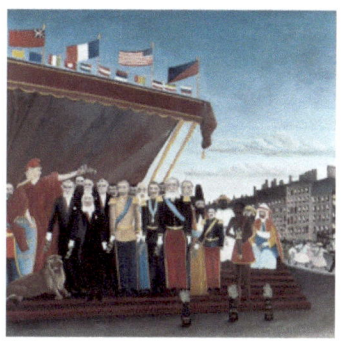 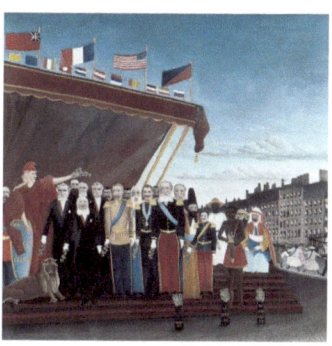

 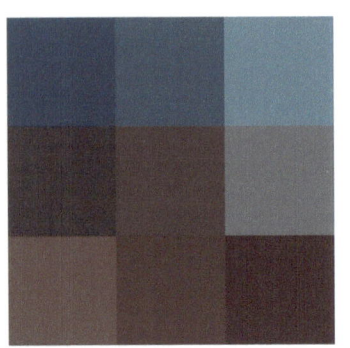 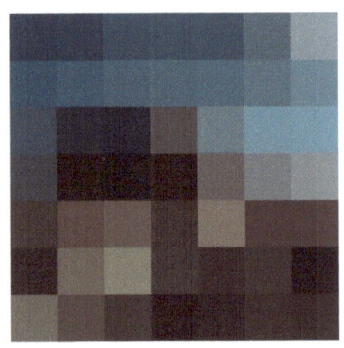

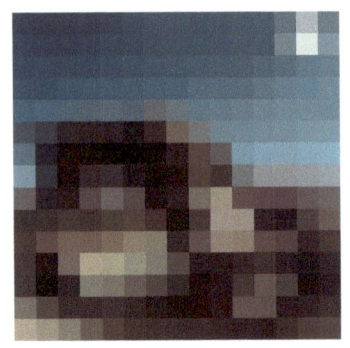 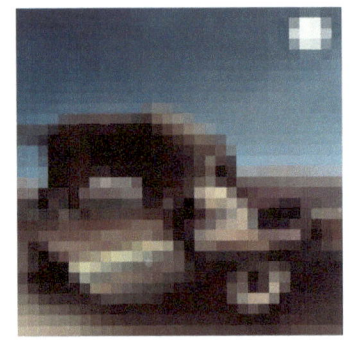 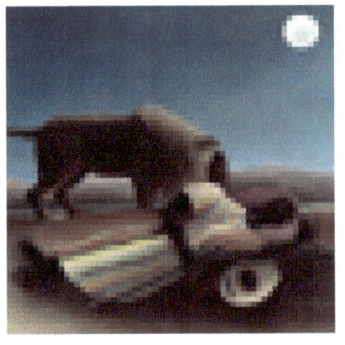

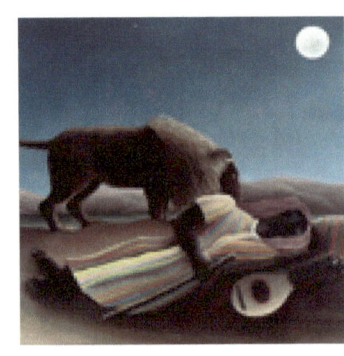 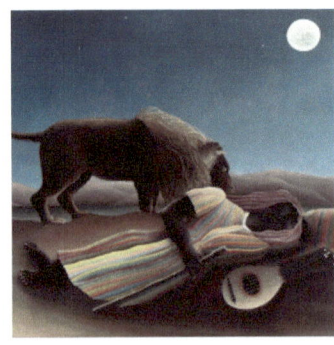 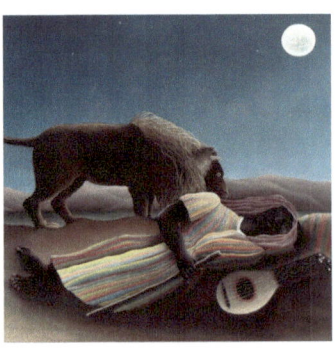

 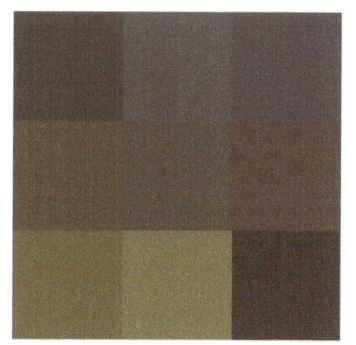 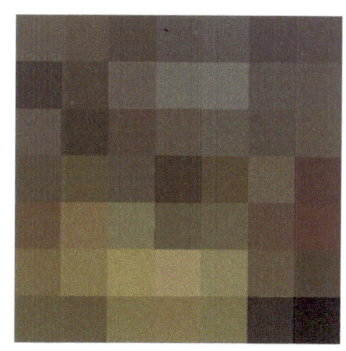

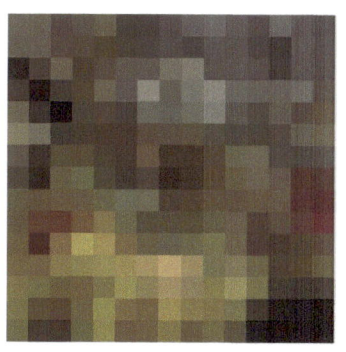 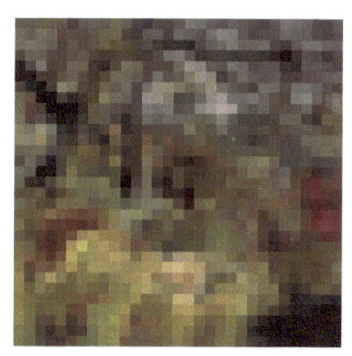 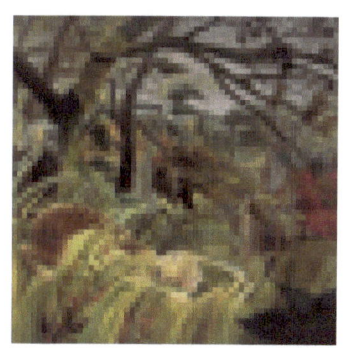

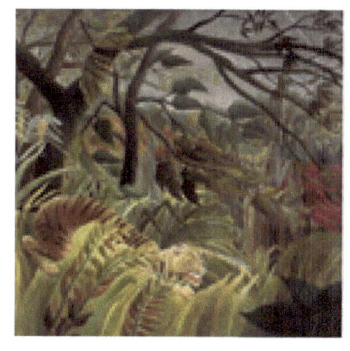 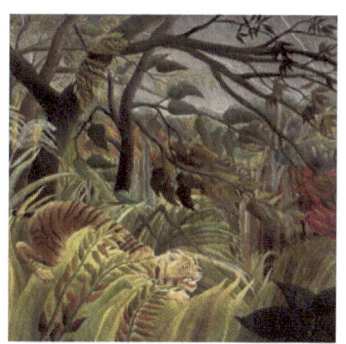 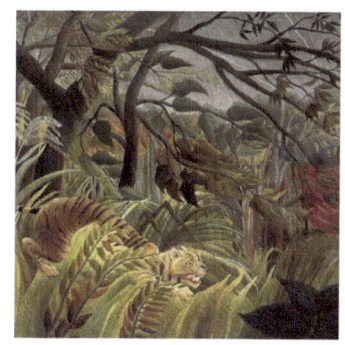

Paul is an American/German artist and the author of *Codex Optica: An Epic Visual Poem In Three Parts* and the **RECONSTRUCTED** series of art books (*Bosch, Da Vinci, Rembrandt, Vermeer, Monet, Renoir, Cézanne, Van Gogh,* and *Rousseau*) available from:

ANIDIAN

www.anidian.com

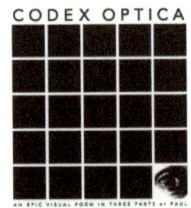 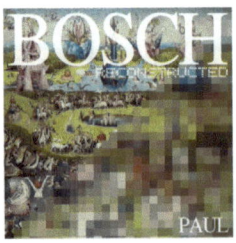 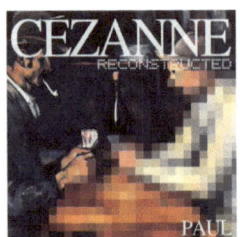 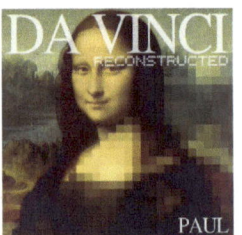 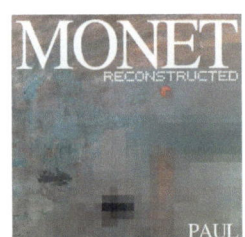

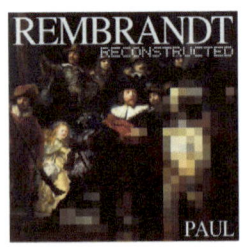 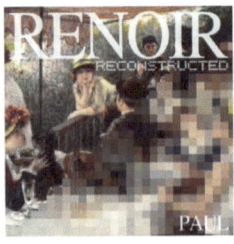 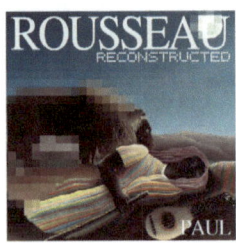 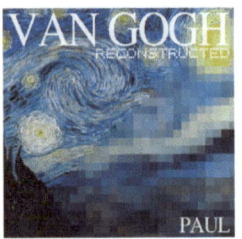 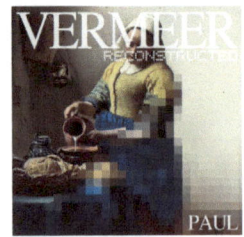

www.ingramcontent.com/pod-product-compliance
Lightning Source LLC
Chambersburg PA
CBHW050851180526
45159CB00007B/2637